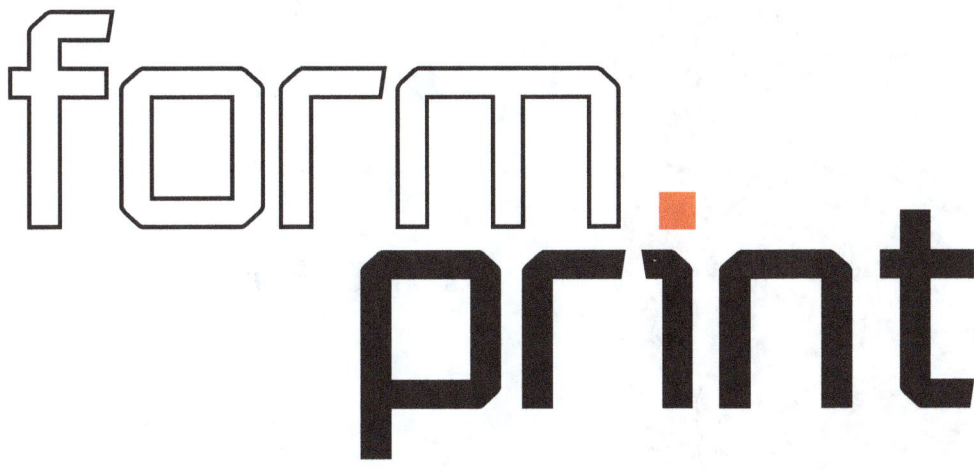

form print

Center for the Arts Gallery
February 1, 2019 - April 20, 2019

Center for the Arts Gallery, Towson University
8000 York Road
Towson, Maryland 21252
Copyright © 2020

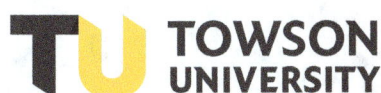
TU TOWSON UNIVERSITY

This exhibition was supported in part by the following:

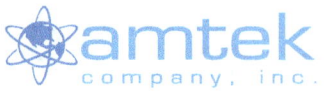

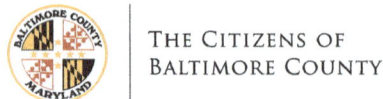

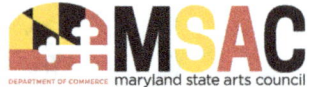

MSAC
maryland state arts council

ISBN 9781716730511
Library of Congress Control Number
2020913560

Logo design: Scott Spector

J. Susan Isaacs, Editor
Joshua DeMonte, Author

Catalogue design: Margot Van Den Berghe

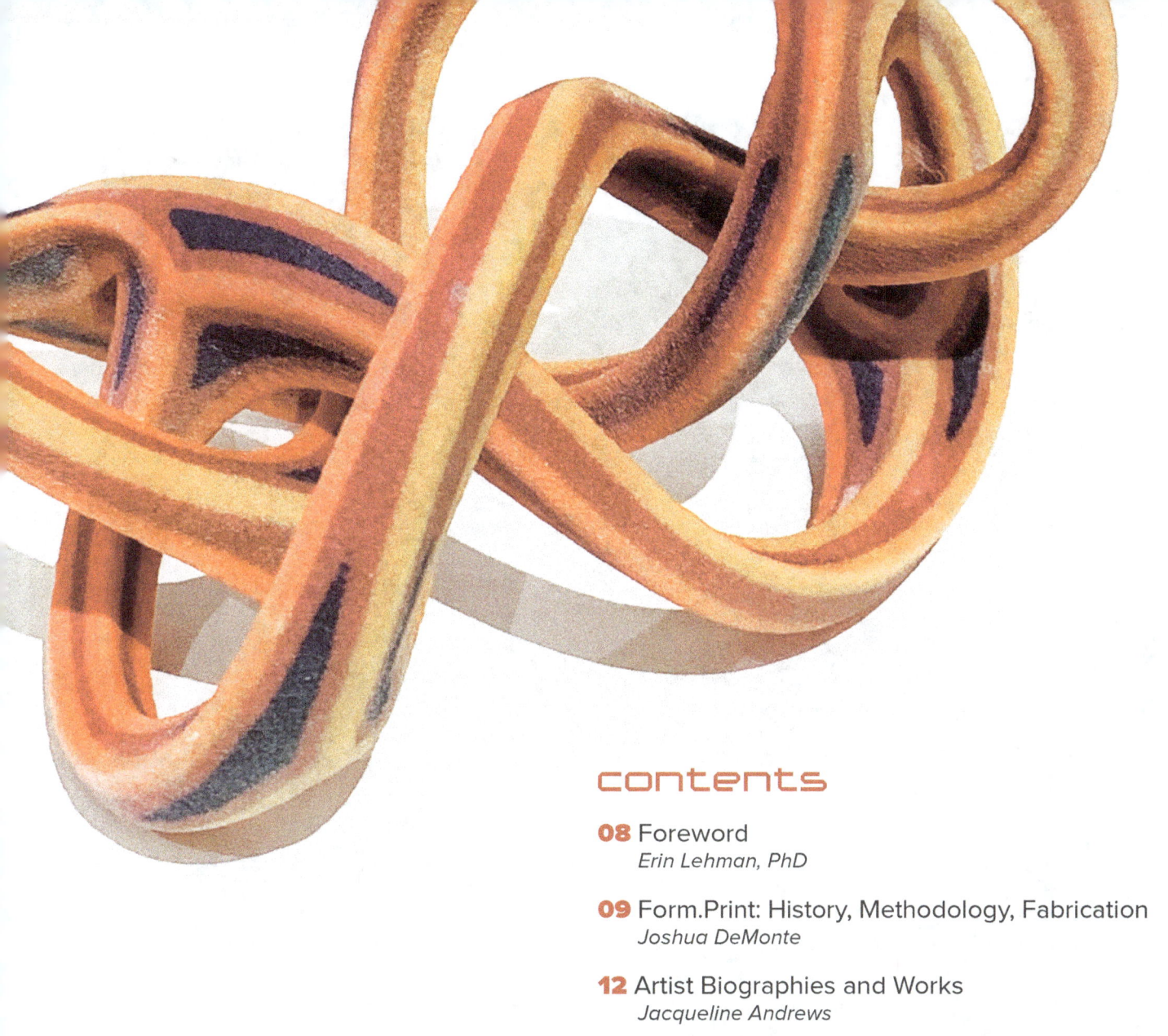

contents

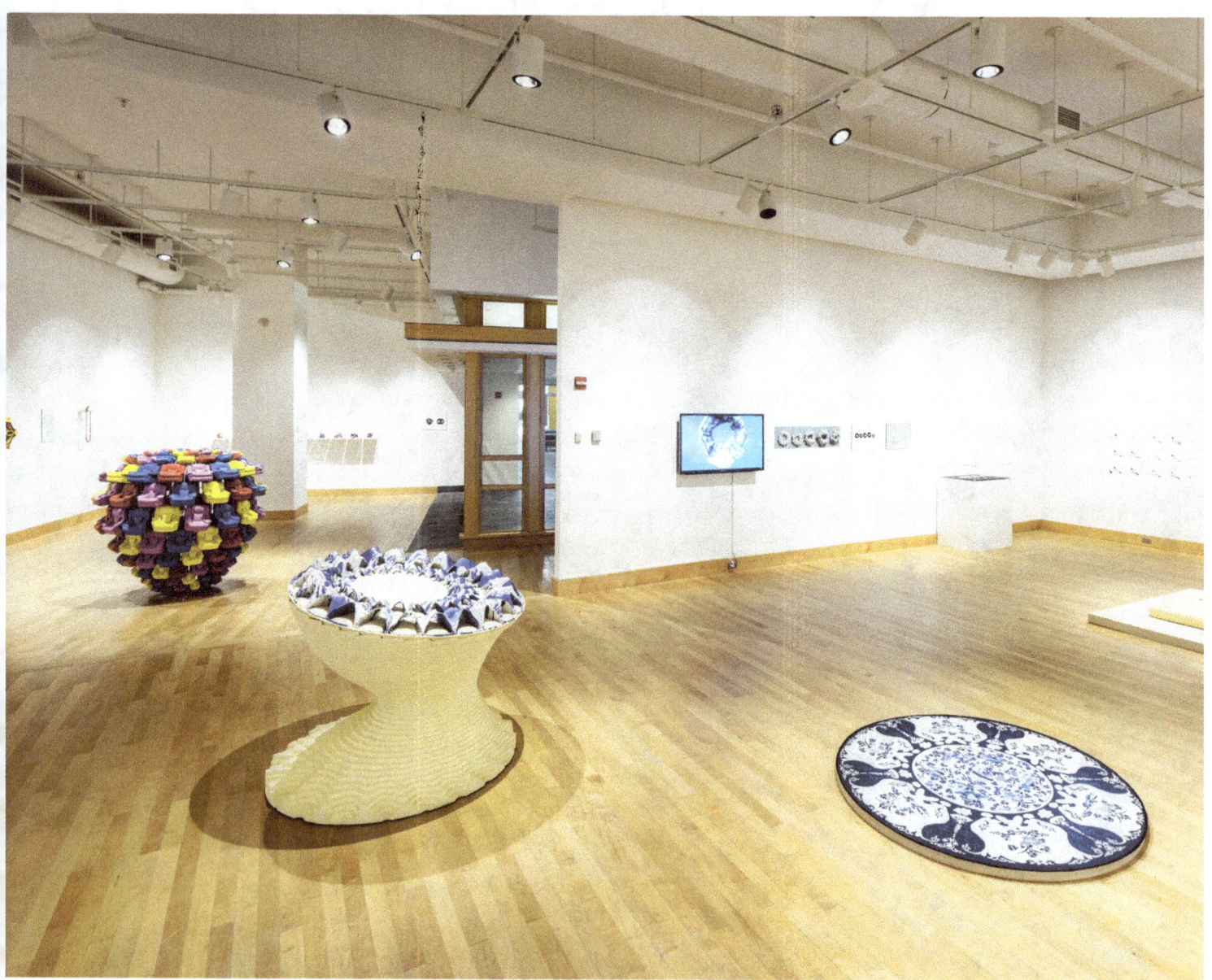

Form.Print, Installation View. Photographs by Dan Meyers

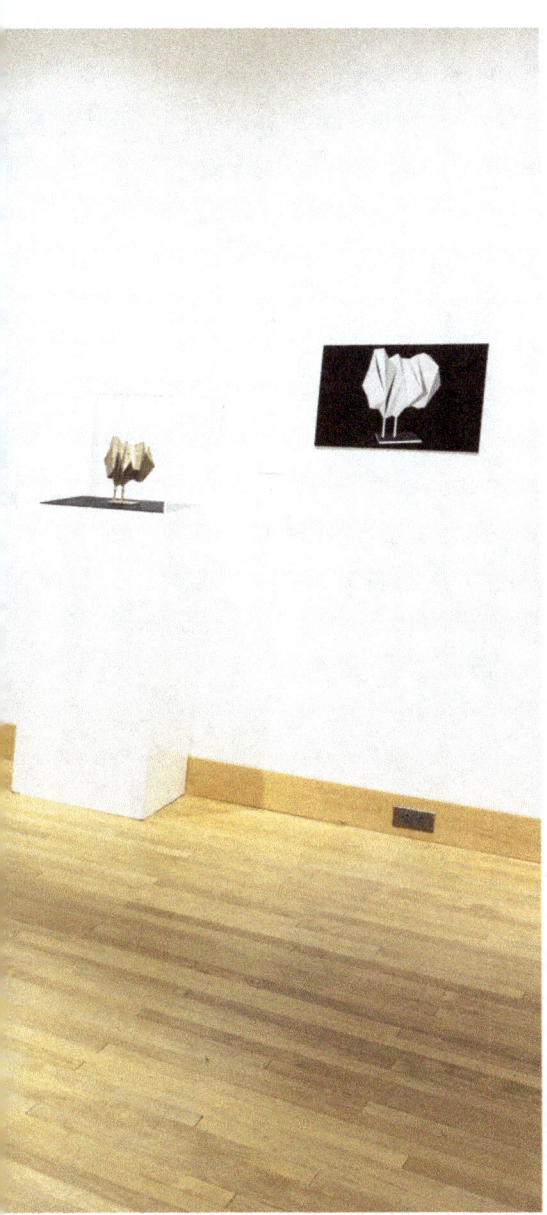

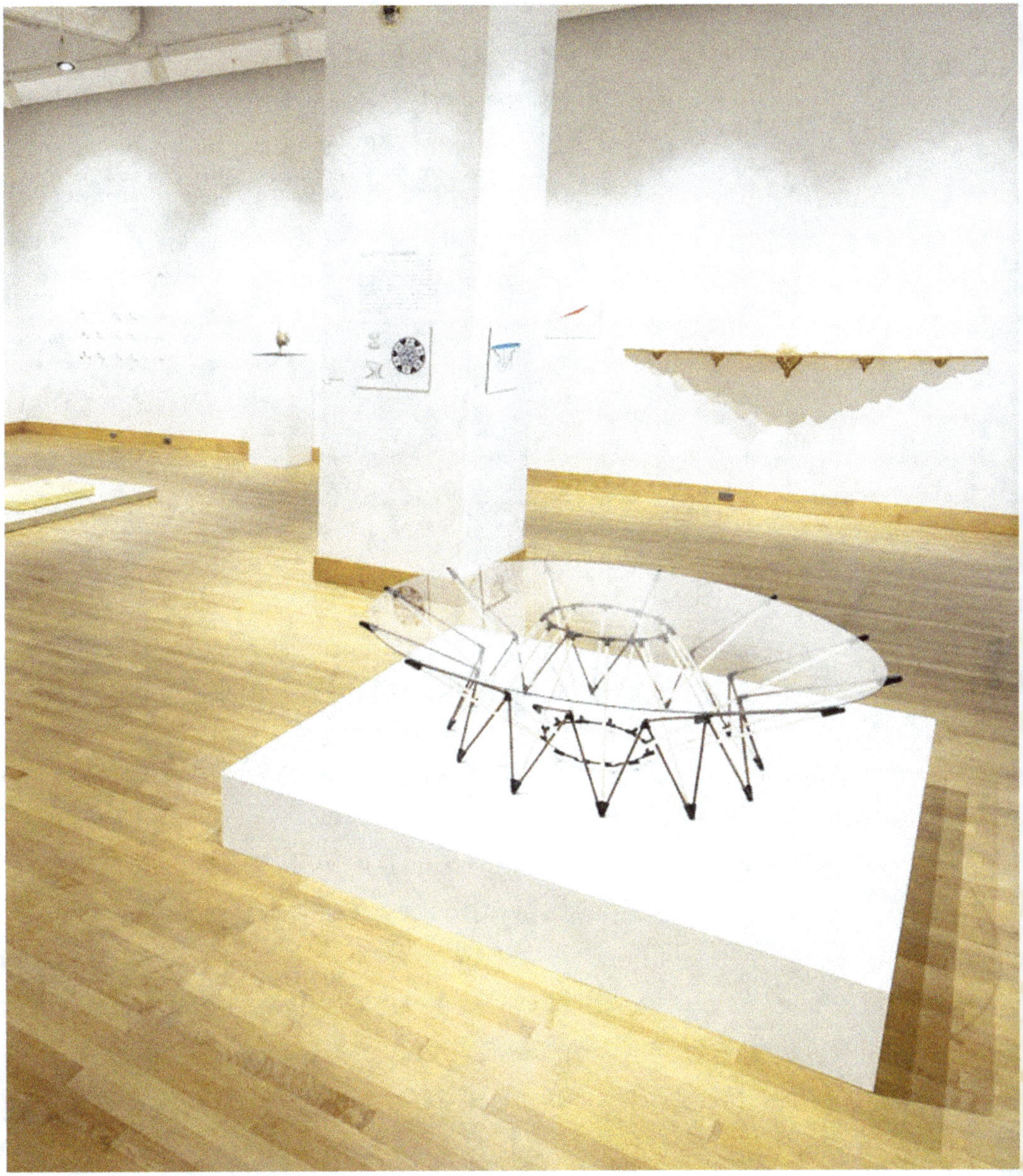

foreword

Like all successful art and all true technological advances, it began as an idea. It became an experiment, a leap into the unknown, a challenge for the invited artists as well as for the curator, faculty, staff, and students in the gallery and in the digital fabrication lab at Towson University. The concept was straightforward: invite artists to test the unedited potential of additive and subtractive digital tools. And test them they did. Computer files became, through the tireless effort of *Form.Print* curator, Joshua DeMonte, and his determined students, physical beings: complicated, beautiful, sometimes whimsical, and always thought-provoking artworks.

In choosing to celebrate the sometimes fraught historical relationship between art and technology, this exhibition revealed the potentialities of collaboration among disciplines, and between sometimes far-flung parties—artist and operator, concept and object, vision and fruition. The lessons learned, and the outcomes achieved here, are a testament to both the incredible possibilities inherent in 3-D technologies, and to the ways in which humans navigate the limits of such technology.

Many thanks to the artists, faculty, staff, and students who agreed to take this leap with us. Your combined talent, ingenuity, and flexibility made *Form.Print* come to life. This exhibition was made possible with support, both financial and institutional, from the Maryland State Arts Council; The Baltimore County Commission on Arts and Sciences; Susan E. Picinich, Dean of the College of Fine Arts and Communication; Jenee Mateer, Chair of the Department of Art + Design, Art History, Art Education; Dr. J. Susan Isaacs, Curator of the Department's Galleries; Michael Bouyoucas, art handler and exhibition installer; and Venetia Zachary, Director of the Visual Resource Center. Thank you to all.

Erin Lehman, PhD
Director of the Department of Art + Design, Art History, Art Education Galleries
Towson University

Form.Print: history, methodology, fabrication

Digital fabrication provides us with the ability to treat objects as information. The capacity to transmit information across space and time stretches as far back as the invention of the telegraph. Over the last half-century, the need and desire for such technology has led to rapid-fire invention, first of the fax machine and its like, and then more recently, the ability to digitally share music, movies, and games. With the proliferation of 3-D printers, the sharing of three-dimensional objects is possible. *Form.Print* explored the idea of treating art as information and instruction. Artists in craft, fine arts, and design provided virtual models, in the form of digital files that represented their artistic vision. The artwork then came to final fruition in Towson University's Object Lab, and other TU locations, using the directions of the artist, with the result a true collaboration between maker, operator, and machine. TU students and faculty worked together to fabricate the objects. Each tangible work was exhibited alongside an initial drawing, further illuminating the relationship between technology, art, and artistic vision. This exhibition demonstrated how our advances into the digital allow for the transmission of sophisticated information—information that directly resulted in concrete form.

Ultimately, eighteen artists submitted original works through digital files, and over the course of six months, the faculty, students, and staff used the technology at TU to produce the pieces. The artists, their works, and the fabrication processes that led up to the show were selected with three elements in mind: that the work represented a valuable or meaningful example of a key concept within digital fabrication philosophies; that it demonstrated a dynamic or innovative use of technology; and finally, that it showed a unique perspective from a specific field or practice. Not all of the artists in this exhibition are technology wizards. Some are heavily or exclusively engaged in digital workflows, while others have a practice where the digital bears the same significance as the hacksaw or MIG welder. For them, it is simply a tool.

The planning process was complex. It began with drafting a list of all technology available to us on campus and producing an outline of the materials, scales, and finishes that could be executed. We offered our participating artists generous options. On the plus side, the extensive list resulted in a diverse exhibition with ambitious work. On the other hand, it became difficult to keep track of complicated fabrications and extensive material lists.

HERE IS WHAT WE OFFERED TO THE ARTISTS:

Zcorp, Zprinter 250
Material: Plaster, Urethane Resin or Cyanoacrylate
Maximum Single Part Dimensions: 9"x7"x5"

Objet, Desktop 30
Material: Veroblue or other opaque object materials possible
Maximum Single Part Dimensions: 11.5" x 7.5" x 5.5"

Formlabs, Form 2
Material: Grey, Clear, White, Black, Flexible
Maximum Single Part Dimensions: 5.7"x5.7"x6.9"

Makerbot, Gen 5
Material: PLA (Any reliable, sourceable PLA available)
Maximum Single Part Dimensions: 11.6"x7.6"x6.5"

Universal Laser, PLS4.75
Material: All sourceable CO2 laser compatible materials
Maximum Cutting Area: 24"x18"

Torchmate, CNC Plasma Torch
Material: 11 – 20-gauge steel
Maximum Cutting Area: 36"x40"

Shopbot, PRSalpha
Material: Most common sourceable router materials.
Maximum Cutting Area: 4'x8'

Solidscape, 3Z Studio
Material: wax to sourceable bronze, limited sterling silver
Maximum Cutting Area: 6"x6"x2"
(maximum build size not desired)

Zencut, Vinyl Cutter
Material: Removable indoor vinyl (preferred source is US cutter)
Maximum Cutting Width: 22"

Many colleagues across TU contributed to the fabrication of the works: Suzanne Obenshain and Deborah Fuller, School of Education; Robert Cave and Matt Wynd, Office of Technology Services; Anthony Rosas; Department of Theater Arts; and thank you to Megan Bradshaw and Henry Basta, University Communications, who documented the exhibition project on film.

As the work was submitted, we began evaluating the files. This entailed attempting to project material consumption, confirming viability, and establishing step-by-step workflows. The diversity of the show was certainly a benefit to the final exhibition but also resulted in a large spectrum of files and organizational systems.

Some artists provided exacting schematics and staged instructions for the work, while others embraced the hands-off possibilities and allowed for in-process decision making as you would expect in a personal studio practice. Production became an astounding responsibility. We set off prepping files, printing, cutting, and assembling.

I am proud of the level of dedication, advanced problem solving, and respect that both the immediate student exhibition team and the students in the program demonstrated. As I dove head first down the rabbit hole, it was fulfilling as both an educator and collaborator to see my students and, in this case, colleagues, unblinkingly dive in with me.

First and foremost, digital fabrication possesses uniquely unlimited form potential. Unlike its predecessors, which are frequently labeled "traditional" tools or analog processes, the combination of technologies under the digital fabrication umbrella result in the ability to yield any physical form. As an educator, I push my students to consider how this mode of working allows for form language that is not possible with other tool sets. I ask them to consider how we can use the process to yield forms that are completely new or unique to this process.

sThe form-potential argument relies heavily on an oversimplified thought experiment in which money is no object, all technology is immediately available, and all artists can deploy any skills masterfully on command. This is clearly a sliding scale, but we can, at the very least, appreciate the demonstration of potentials that yield unique or unseen outcomes.

A discussion of the ideas of mass production, mass variability, and mass customization, as with the form argument, relies on the combination of technologies in the digital fabrication family. In traditional manufacturing, most components and products rely on custom tooling (most commonly molds and dies) and machines to continuously produce copies of these components or products. This directly inhibits variation. Tooling is extraordinarily expensive and with each new form a new mold, die, or tool is needed. 3-D printers and CNC mills do not rely on tooling for production. Each technology in these families has a specific set of parameters they operate within, and from there can produce any form within those constraints. This allows each form produced to be unique. These distinctive forms span from objects individually crafted with specific intent to objects born from an algorithm that is manipulated by an artist, the consumer, or another machine.

Indirect processes include simulation, generation, and scanning. A close relative to mass customization is the generative powers of the computer. Simulations, scripts and programs, and scanning technologies allow artists and users to create with parameters instead of objective constructive actions. There is plenty of evidence of this in the analogue, such as Tehching Hsieh's *Time Clock Piece* (1980-81) where the artist punched a timecard every hour on the hour for one year. The computer has given us a few new potentials, though the principles behind this idea are not new. Technology can now deploy these ideas. Fifteen years ago, a whole farm of computers would work for days to generate one of these simulations where now a single computer can tackle the same amount in a day.

Participating national and international artists included Rebecca Annand, Doug Bucci, Emily Cobb, Annet Couwenberg, Emily Culver, Lisa Dillin, Maria Eife, Bathsheba Grossman, Del Harrow, Ryan Mandell, Julian Mayor, Annika Pettersson, Phillip Renato, J. Alex Schechter, Eric Standley, Chris Boyd Taylor, Katja Toporski, and Colin Wiencek. While *Form.Print* was a huge undertaking for our faculty, staff, and students, it was an exceptional experience that resulted in a momentary vision of digital processes in craft, fine arts, and design.

Joshua DeMonte
Curator of Form.Print

REBECCA ANNAND

Rebecca Annand works in both metal and plastic using 3-D technologies to create wearable pieces. She employs texture and repetition as a descriptor, wrapping space with pattern. The shell expands and contracts in density as it undulates and takes on new contours, describing what is not there. She comments, "The first form of art I ever loved was blind contour drawing... While I have most definitely left simplicity behind, the value of describing space through means other than direct render has stayed with me. In this new study, pen and paper have been traded in favor of computer-aided modeling and additive printing." Her current body of work is derived primarily from historic cameo and intaglio forms. Since 2010, she has worked as a design professional in New York City, specializing in luxury fashion and couture jewelry design. Her work has been included in exhibitions at the Mint Museum, Charlotte, North Carolina; Old Courthouse Art Center, Woodstock, Illinois; Arkansas Arts Center, Little Rock; Crane Arts, Philadelphia, Pennsylvania; and The Jung Center, Houston, Texas. It has also been included in the pages of *American Craft Magazine* and *500 Enameled Objects* (Lark Books). Annand holds both MFA and BFA in Metals/Jewelry/CAD-CAM from the Tyler School of Art and Architecture at Temple University.

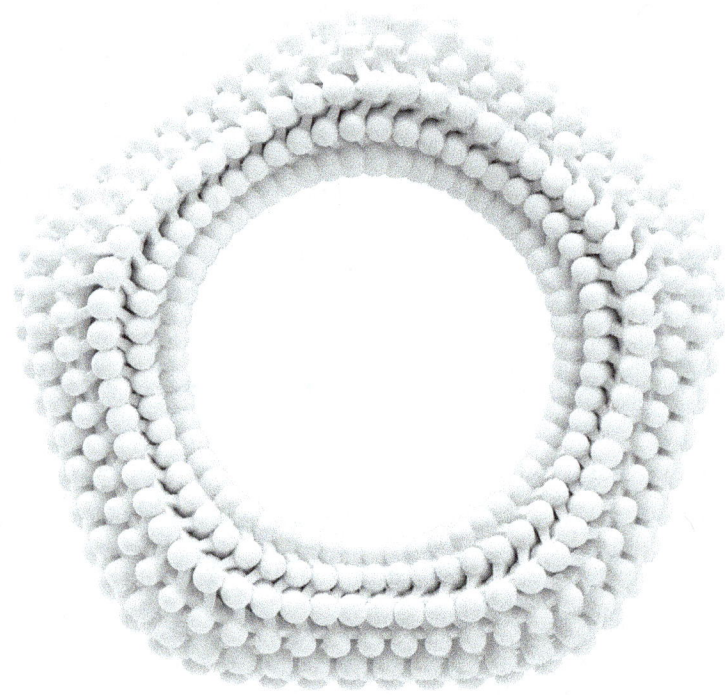

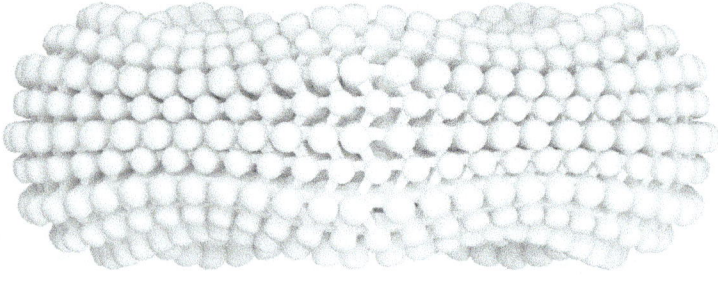

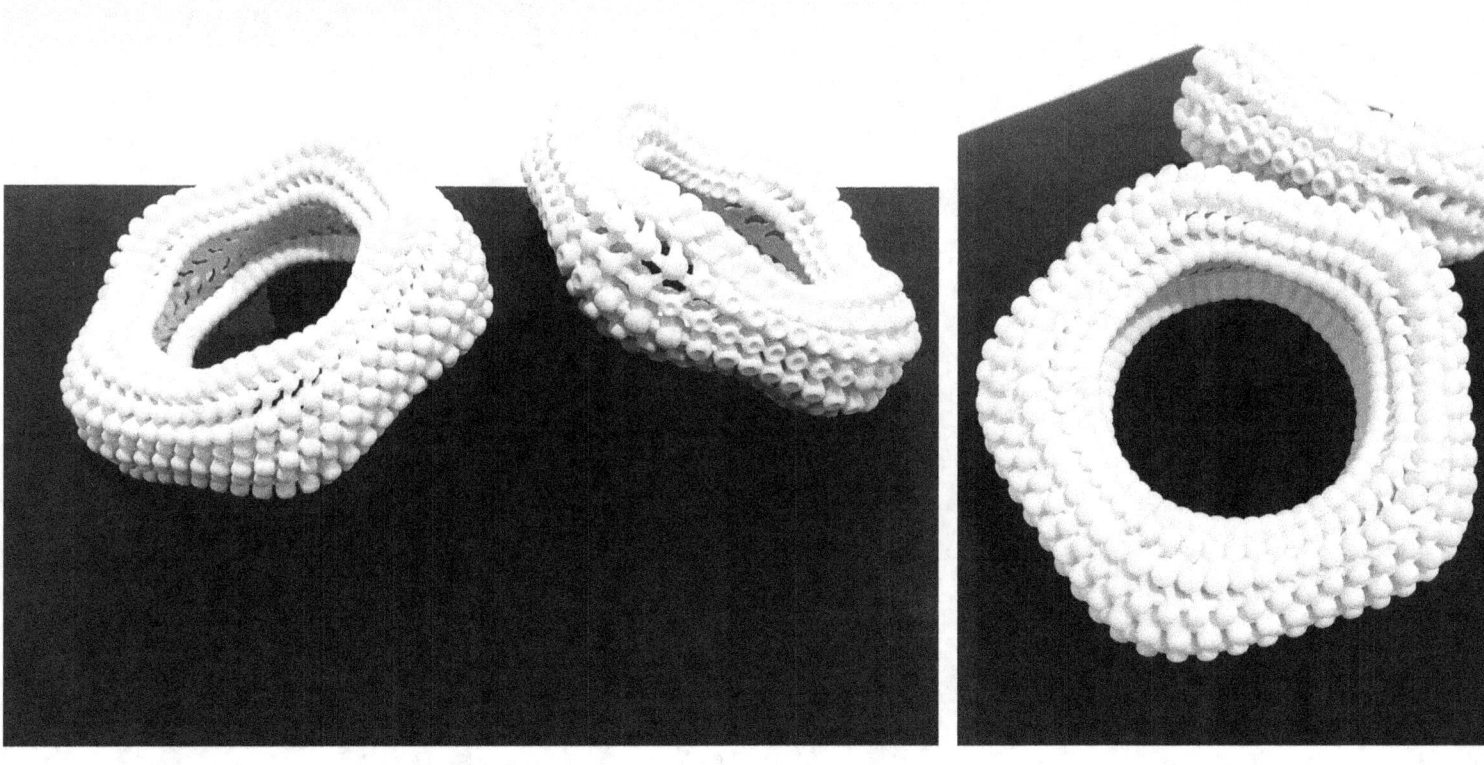

Rebecca Annand, *Surface Scapes Study One* and *Study Two*, 2018
Gypsum, epoxy resin

DOUG BUCCI

Doug Bucci is a jewelry and object designer who utilizes digital processes and CAD technologies to create work that transcends the confines of traditional handwork in jewelry fabrication. He explores biology and the effect of disease on the body. CAD technologies allow Bucci to simulate and transform biological patterns and forms into meaningful and deeply personal wearables and objects. He has exhibited with numerous museums and institutions nationally and internationally, including the Cooper Hewitt Smithsonian Design Museum, New York; the Philadelphia Museum of Art and the Wayne Art Center, both in Pennsylvania; the Museum of Arts and Design, New York; the Museum of Fine Arts, Boston, Massachusetts; the Designmuseo, Helsinki, Finland; the State Hermitage Museum, St. Petersburg, Russia; the Estonian Museum of Applied Art and Design, Tallinn, Estonia; National Gallery of Victoria, Melbourne, Australia; and the Design Museum, London, England. His work is in the permanent collections of the Cooper Hewitt Smithsonian Design Museum, New York; Philadelphia Museum of Art, Pennsylvania; Los Angeles County Museum of Art, California; Yale University Art Gallery, New Haven, Connecticut; Susan Grant Lewin Collection, Georgia Museum of Fine Arts, Athens; Newark Museum, New Jersey; Ilias Lalaounis Jewelry Museum, Athens, Greece; Helen Williams Drutt Collection, National Gallery of Australia, Canberra; Pinakothek der Moderne, Munich and Goldschmiedehaus, Hanau, both in Germany; Design Museo, Helsinki, Finland; State Hermitage Museum, St. Petersburg, Russia; and the collections of Windsor Castle, Berkshire, England. His work has been featured in multiple publications, including the Lark Craft's *500* Series texts, *Crafted: Objects in Flux*, a publication of the Museum of Fine Arts in Boston, Massachusetts; *American Craft* magazine, and *Metalsmith* magazine, in which Bucci's own writing has also been published. He has written numerous articles for *Art Jewelry Forum*. He is the Program Head of the Metals/Jewelry/CAD-CAM program at Tyler School of Art and Architecture at Temple University in Philadelphia, Pennsylvania. Bucci received an MFA in Metals/Jewelry/CAD-CAM from Tyler School of Art and Architecture and a BFA from The University of the Arts, Philadelphia. He is represented by Sienna Patti Contemporary, Lenox, Massachusetts.

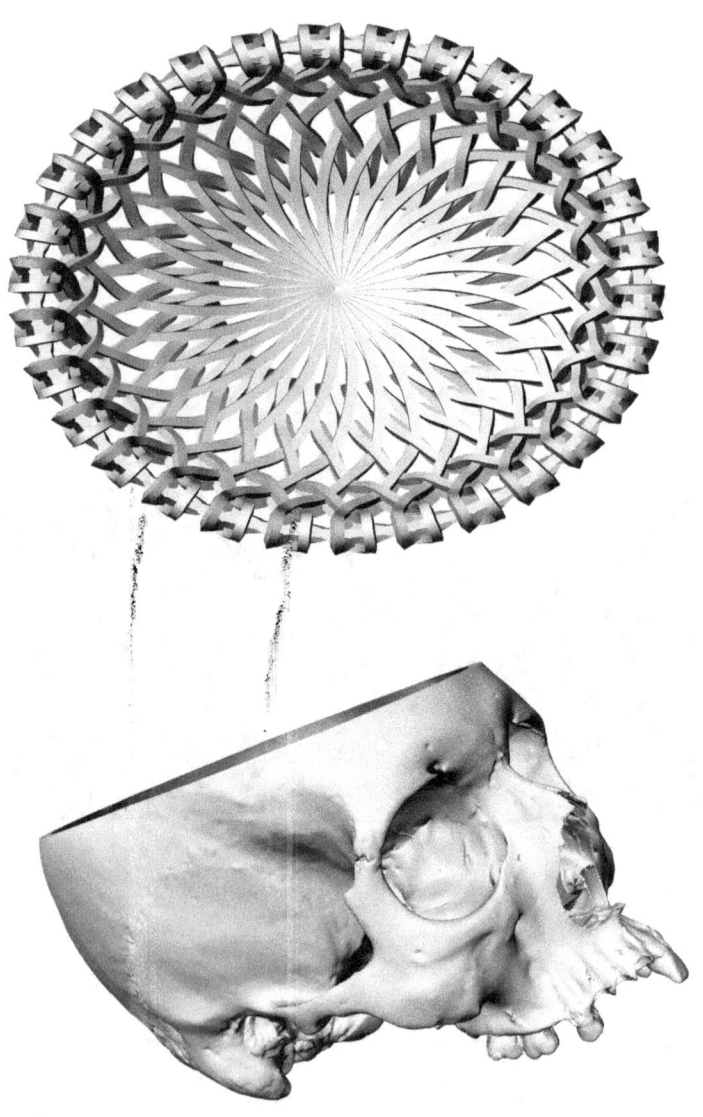

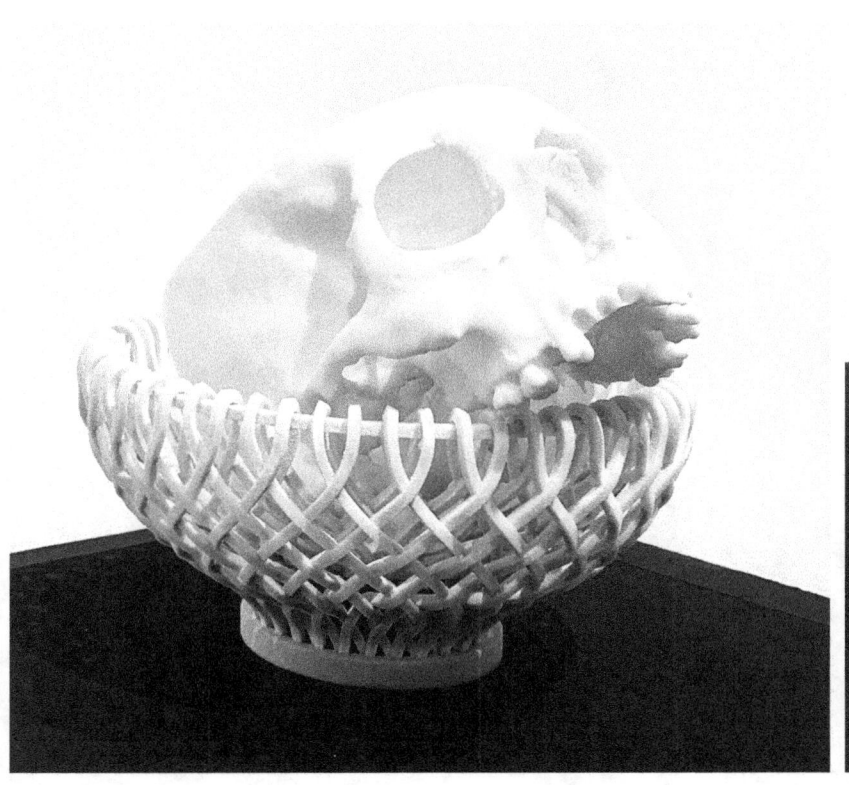
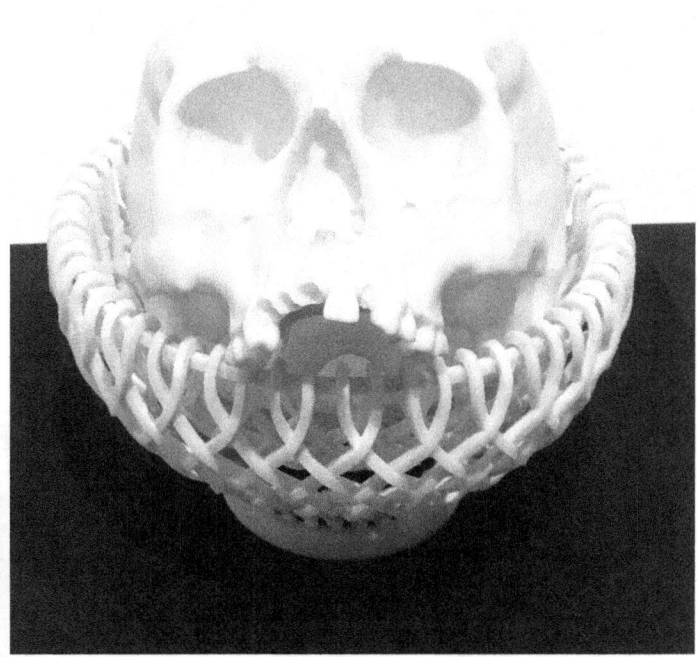

Doug Bucci, *Sugar Bowl,* 2018
Gypsum, photopolymer resin, epoxy resin

EMILY COBB

Emily Cobb is a jewelry designer and maker who utilizes both digital technology and traditional fabrication techniques. She creates her jewelry from personal fables that often contain animals as central parts of the imagery. Cobb is moved by living things that change over time. Her latest work is inspired by wooden snake toys. Her pieces slither around the neck and torso with bold patterns that represent specific snake species. Their bright designs lure the viewer, with color as "an innocent temptress... a seductive force... a sensual display." She further comments: "When the body becomes part of the composition it animates the work, and I want this interaction to spark creative discussion and dialog." In addition to a solo exhibition at the Philadelphia Art Alliance, she has exhibited at numerous museums including The Delaware Contemporary (formerly the Delaware Center for the Contemporary Arts), Wilmington; the Racine Art Museum, Wisconsin; and the Bellevue Arts Museum, Washington. Her work has been featured on the cover of *Metalsmith magazine* and in publications such as *Digital Handmade: Craftsmanship in the New Industrial Revolution* (Thames & Hudson). She received a Humanities & Arts Research Fellowship, Temple University-Wagner Free Institute of Science, and an InLiquid Micro-Grant in collaboration with Blick Art Supplies. Cobb is a founding member of JV Collective, a collaborative jewelry group based in South Philadelphia. She is Assistant Professor in Jewelry and Small Metals at Humboldt State University in California. Cobb received both her BFA and MFA in Metals/Jewelry/CAD-CAM from the Tyler School of Art and Architecture at Temple University, Philadelphia, Pennsylvania. She is represented by Sienna Patti Contemporary, Lenox, Massachusetts.

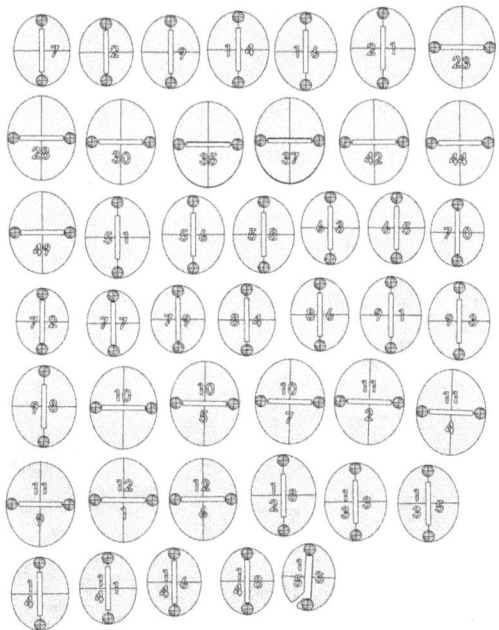

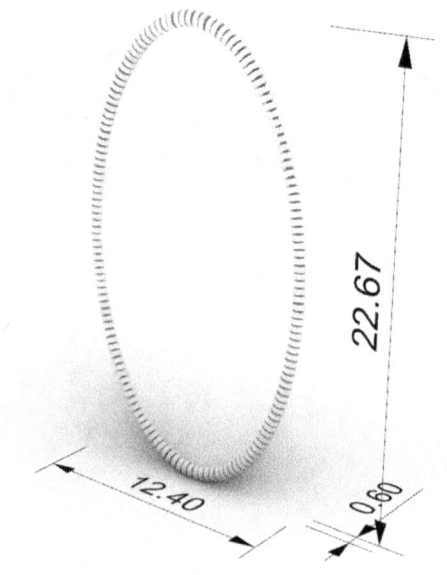

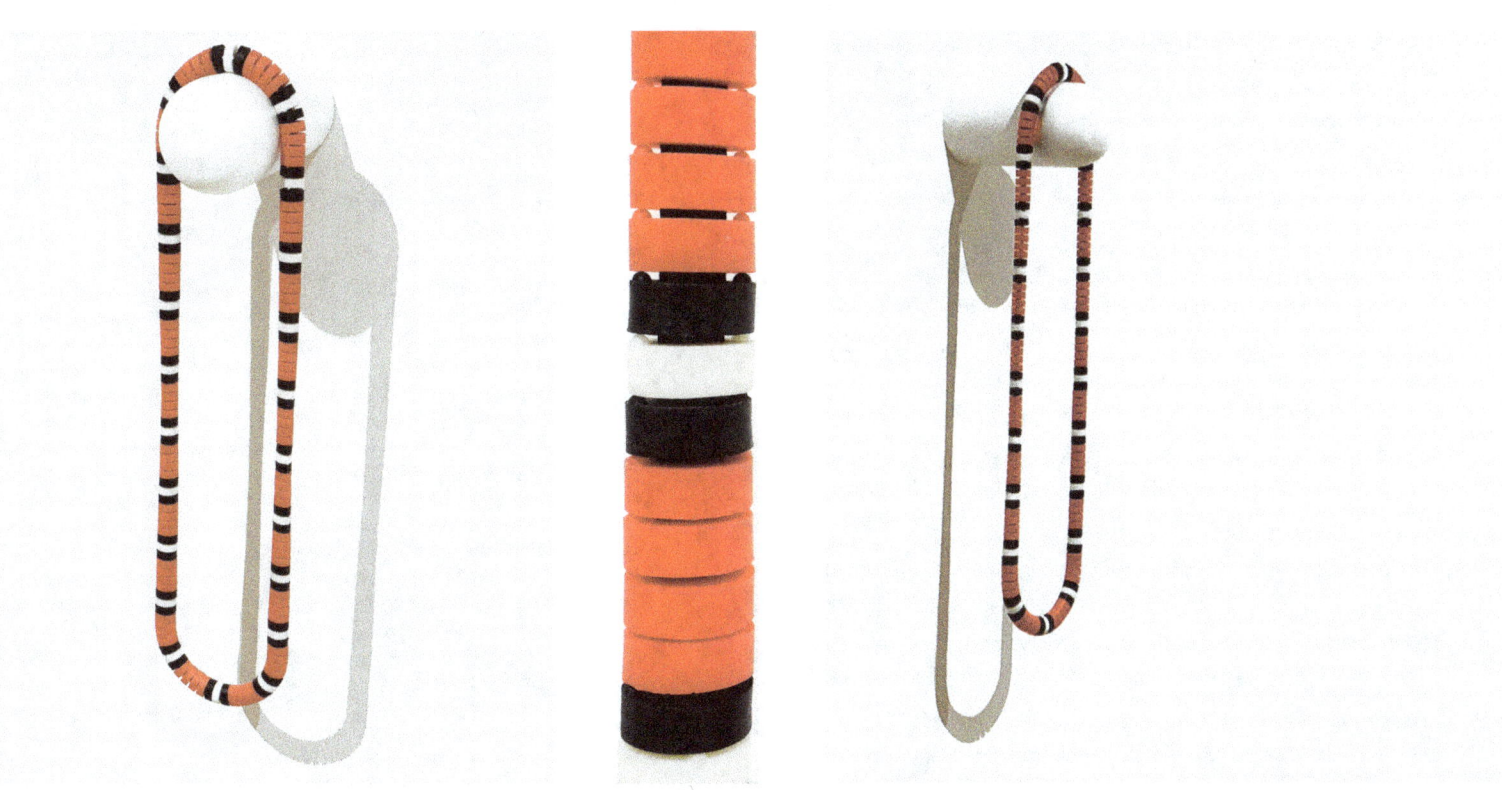

Emily Cobb, *Red Milk XL,* 2018
Photopolymer resin, ribbon

ANNET COUWENBERG

Annet Couwenberg was born in the Netherlands. From her early career in fashion, to her later shift to sculpture and, more recently, to digital media, she remains committed to an interdisciplinary approach, searching out new sources and stimuli, never losing touch with her Dutch textile background. She comments, "My goal as an artist and instructor, through research of traditional textiles and emerging techniques, is to create a multi-directional exchange of knowledge." Her recent subject matter is of fish fossils and skeletons inspired by her study with a fish scientist during a Smithsonian Fellowship. She has many publications, including a monograph by Telos Art Publishing, and articles and reviews in *The New York Times*; *The Los Angeles Times*; *The Washington Post*; *Le Monde*; *BMoreArt*; the *Baltimore Sun*; *Sculpture Magazine*; *Fiberarts*; *Surface Design Journal*; and *Textile: The Journal of Cloth and Culture*. She has exhibited nationally and internationally, including the Museum of Arts and Design, New York; The Delaware Contemporary (formerly the Delaware Center for the Contemporary Arts), Wilmington; The Contemporary Museum, Baltimore, Maryland; the Decorative Arts Museum, Little Rock, Arkansas; the USC Fisher Museum, Los Angeles, California; Gyeonggi MOMA and HOMA Museum, Seoul, both in Korea; the American Embassy, The Hague, and the Textile Museum, Tilburg, both in the Netherlands. Her work is in the permanent collections of the Baltimore Museum of Art; Textile Museum and the Museum de Kantfabriek, Horst, both in the Netherlands; and Gyeonggi Creation Center and the Jinnam Art and Culture Center, both in Korea. She has been awarded many grants including several Maryland State Arts Council Individual Artist Awards and a Smithsonian Artist and Research Fellowship, Washington, D. C. Couwenberg holds two MFA degrees: Syracuse University, New York and Cranbrook Academy of Art, Bloomfield Hills, Michigan. She is a Professor at the Maryland Institute College of Art, Baltimore.

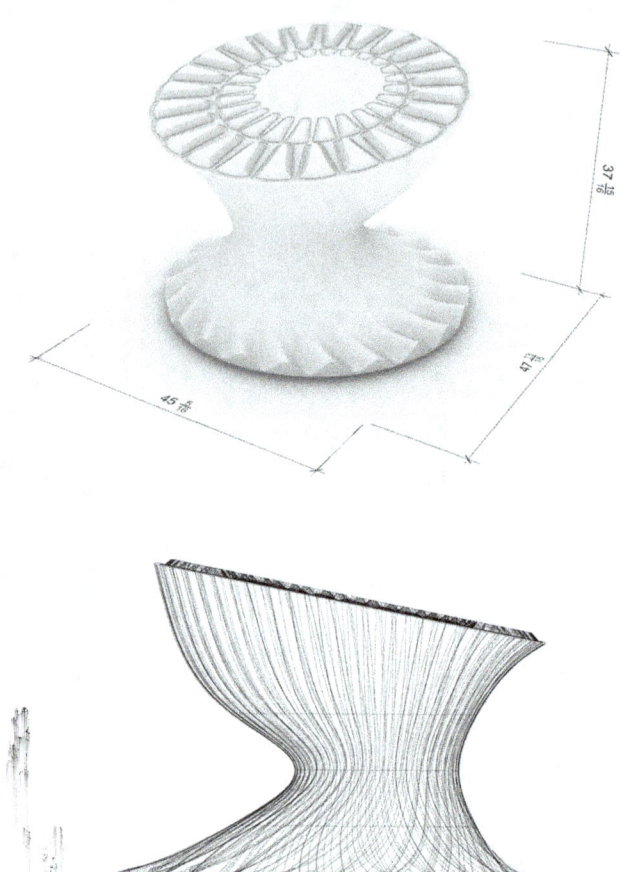

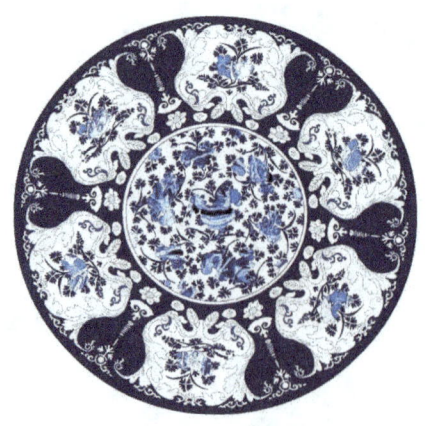

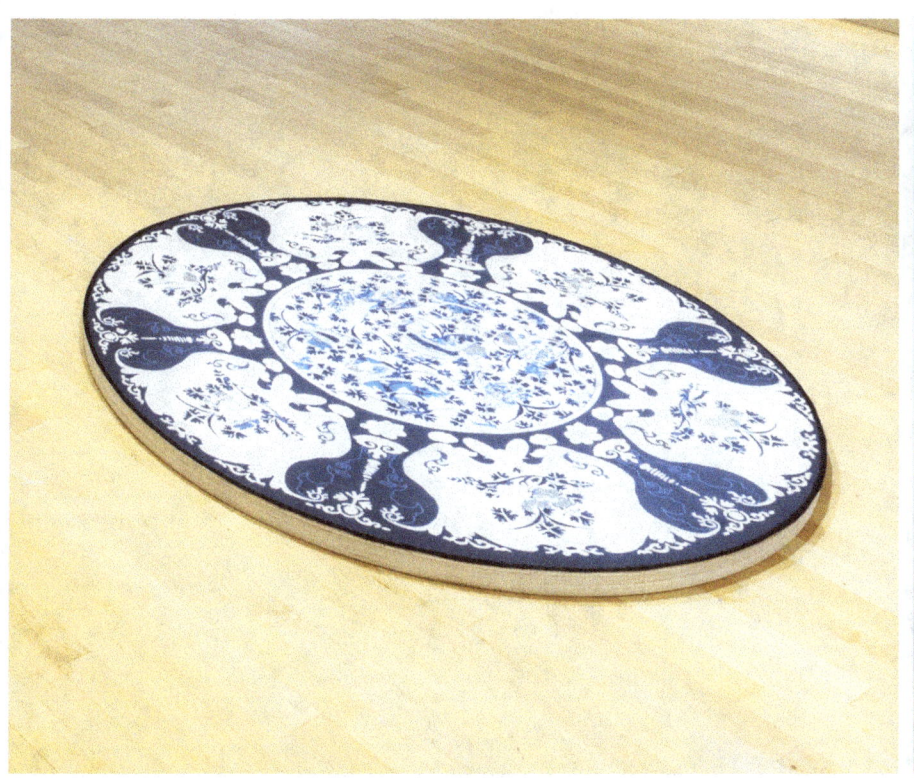

Annet Couwenberg, *Delft Blue no 1 (rug),* 2018
Synthetic
Jacquard woven by EE exclusives in
Heeze, Netherland

Photograph by Dan Meyers

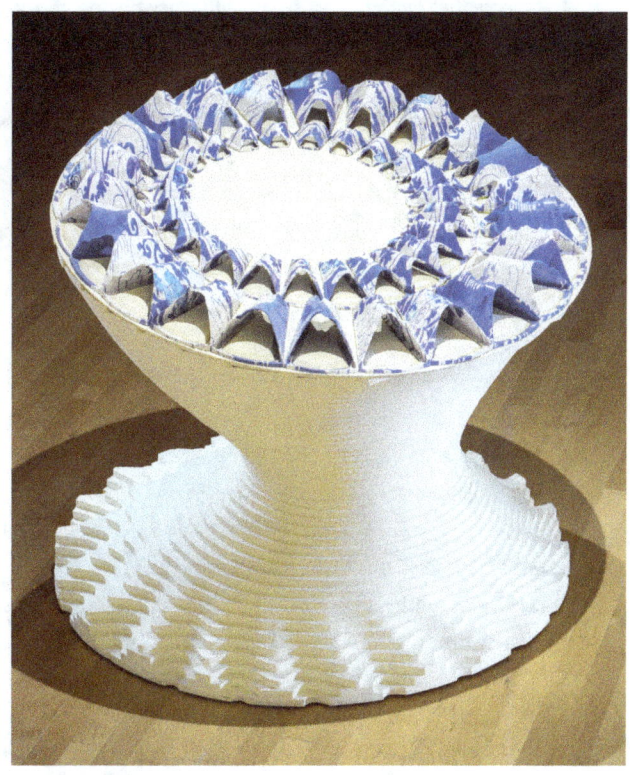

Annet Couwenberg, *Inheritance,* 2018
Plywood, paint, gypsum, epoxy resin
Manufactured at Towson University

Photograph by Dan Meyers

19

EMILY CULVER

Emily Culver is an object maker who utilizes a combination of familiar materials and diverse fabrication techniques drawn from a variety of craft disciplines to create experiential objects that engage and surprise the viewer. She considers her creative practice a "process of trying to understand oneself through intimate interactions with objects." Her forms are meant to evoke existing commonplace objects in order to question their utility and intent. Culver explains: "By presenting familiar communicative affordances—such as handles, vessels, and furniture—in uncharacteristic ways, the viewer is invited to re-frame their own understanding...there is an unveiling and recognition of the viewer's projection of self onto these objects and environments." In addition to a solo exhibition at School 33 Art Center in Baltimore, Maryland, she has shown at galleries and museums across the United States, including Little Berlin Gallery, Philadelphia and Wayne Art Center, both in Pennsylvania; Phoenix Institute of Contemporary Art, Arizona; the Baltimore Jewelry Center, Maryland; Brooklyn Metal Works, New York; the Arrowmont School of Arts and Crafts, Gatlinburg, Tennessee, where she was an Artist-in-Residence; and The Delaware Contemporary (formerly the Delaware Center for the Contemporary Arts), Wilmington. Internationally, she has exhibited with Museum Het Valkhof and Galerie Marzee, both in Nijmegen, the Netherlands. Culver's work has been featured in publications such as *New Rings 2, CAST, AUTOR Magazine,* and *Metalsmith Magazine Shifting Sites*, an Exhibition in Print. She received a Committee's Choice Award from Ethical Metalsmiths, and a Foundation for Contemporary Arts Emergency Grant from the Foundation for Contemporary Arts, New York. Culver has a BFA in Metals/Jewelry/CAD-CAM from Tyler School of Art and Architecture at Temple University and an MFA in Metalsmithing from Cranbrook Academy of Art. She is an instructor in the Craft and Material Studies Department at Virginia Commonwealth University in Richmond, Virginia.

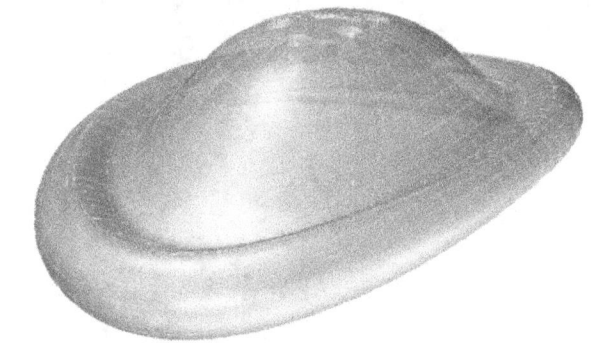

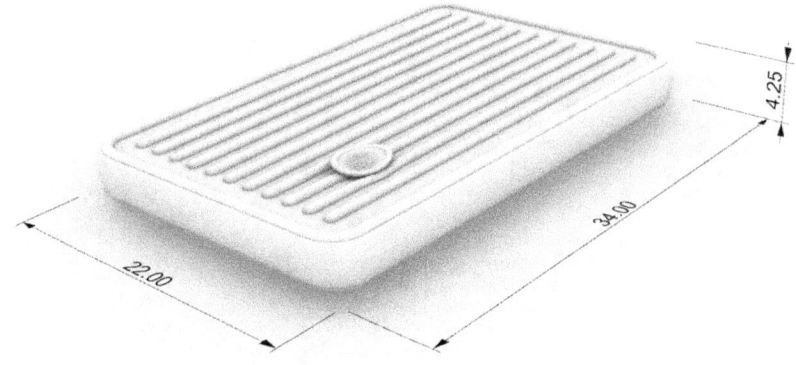

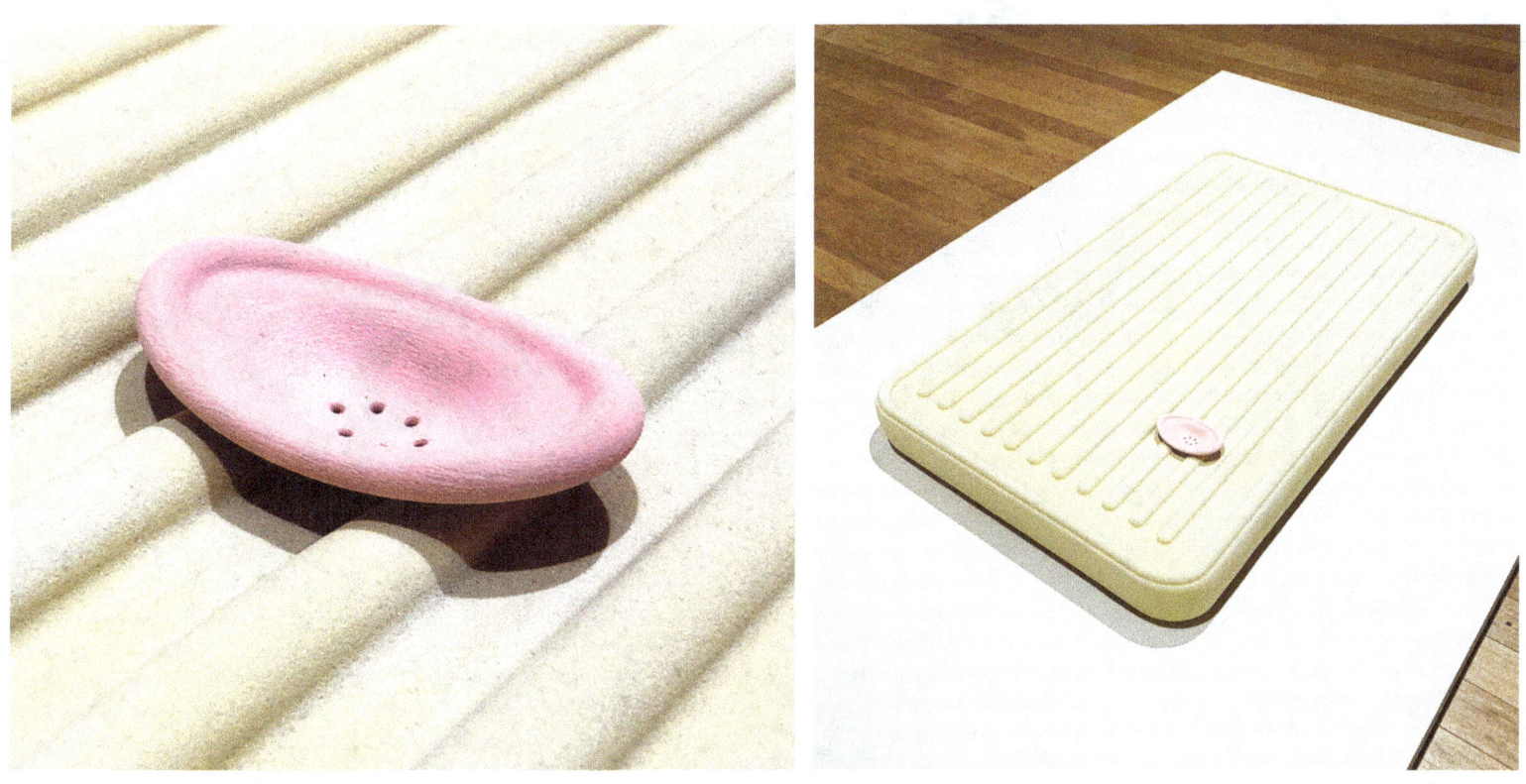

Emily Culver, *Rough Play (Souvenir),* 2018
Modeling foam, gypsum, epoxy resin

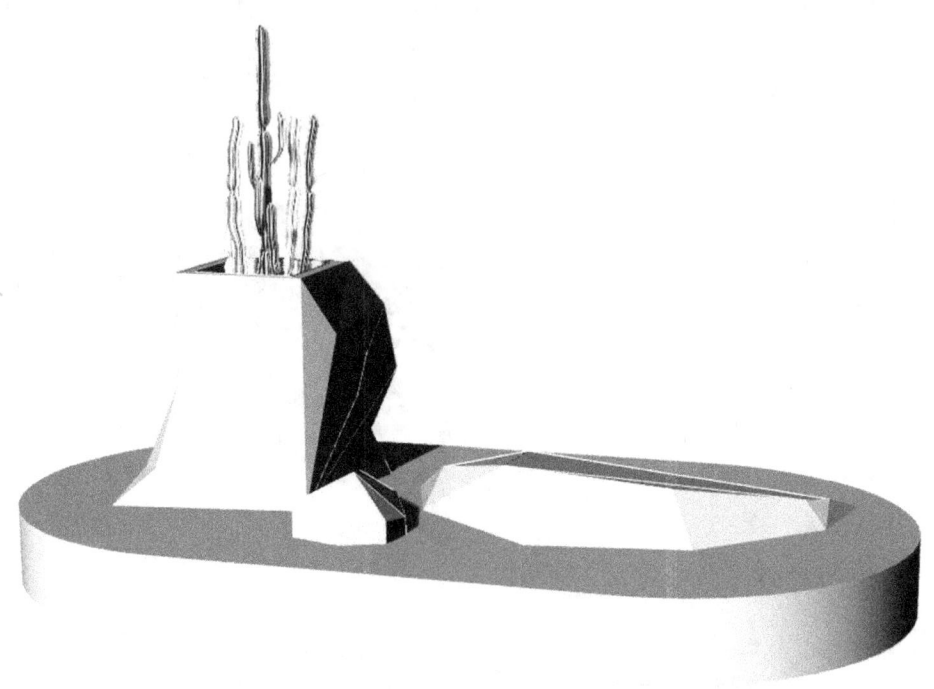

LISA DILLIN

Lisa Dillin is an interdisciplinary artist working in sculpture and experiential art forms. Her work is concerned with human interaction and reaction to the created environment in comparison with the natural world. Dillin explains, "The unattainable goal of replacing our communal experiences of nature with a man-made product is sardonically highlighted as works fail to live up to expectations...I examine human nature: who we were, who we are, and who we strive to become." She has shown her work in many venues including the Baltimore Museum of Art; Silber and Rosenberg Galleries at Goucher College; the Myerhoff and Decker Galleries, Maryland Institute College of Art; and Jordan Faye Contemporary, all in Baltimore, Maryland; Vox Populi, Philadelphia, Pennsylvania; Hamiltonian Gallery, Washington, D.C.; and Cranbrook Art Museum, Bloomfield Hills, Michigan. Dillin has received reviews in *Baltimore Magazine, Bmore Art, Urbanite, The Baltimore Sun, Baltimore City Paper, The Washington Post,* and *Washington City Paper.* She was a Second-Place Finalist for The Trawick Prize, Bethesda, Maryland; a Janet & Walter Sondheim Prize Finalist; and has received two Maryland State Arts Council Individual Artist Awards in Sculpture. She was a recipient of a Hamiltonian Fellowship, Hamiltonian Gallery, Washington, D.C., and her work has been shown at Light City, Baltimore, Maryland; Select Art Fair in New York; Artist-Run Art Fair in Miami, Florida; and (e)merge art fair in Washington, D.C. She has been a faculty member at Pratt Institute and Fashion Institute of Technology, both in New York; Maryland Institute College of Art, Baltimore; American University and Corcoran College of Art + Design, Washington D.C.; and Towson University. Dillin received her BFA in Photography from Atlanta College of Art, Georgia, and her MFA in Sculpture from Cranbrook Academy of Art in Bloomfield Hills, Michigan. She is also the Founder and Program Director of CHM Sculpture Park and Fellowship Program, Baltimore, Maryland.

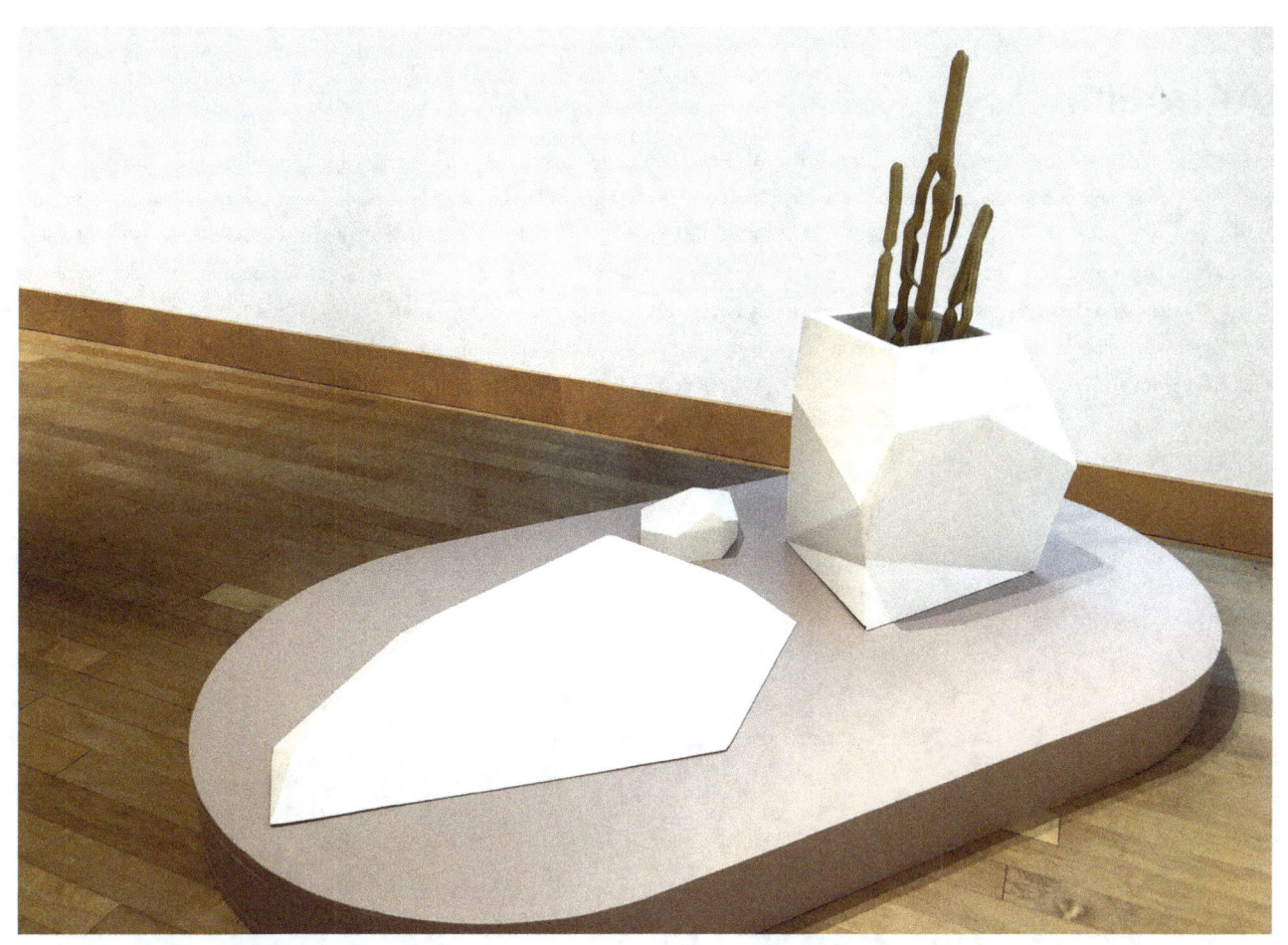

Lisa Dillin, *Equivalent Formations VI,* 2018
Corian, gypsum, epoxy resin, MDF, paint

MARIA EIFE

Maria Eife is a Philadelphia-based jewelry designer and maker who enjoys experimenting with materials and processes and is intrigued by the idea of wearable stories and communication through jewelry. She employs both traditional jewelry methods and newer technologies, including 3-D printing and laser cutting. She comments, "I use 3-D printing and laser cutting to create designs that would be impossible, or extremely expensive to make in any other way. I can recreate the same design over and over or change it slightly and make a series of unique objects. Ultimately, my goal is to create elegant, playful, and structurally complex adornments that complement the wearer and intrigue the viewer." She launched her *Binary Collection*, a line of laser-cut wool felt jewelry using binary code as a design element in 2010. Her work has been featured in *500 Felt Objects* (Lark Books) and *American Craft Magazine*. She was awarded an Editor's Choice Award in the World Maker Faire and has been an invited artist at the American Craft Council Shows, CraftBoston, and the Martha Stewart Holiday Craft Shows. She holds a BFA in Jewelry/Metals/CAD-CAM from the Tyler School of Art and Architecture at Temple University.

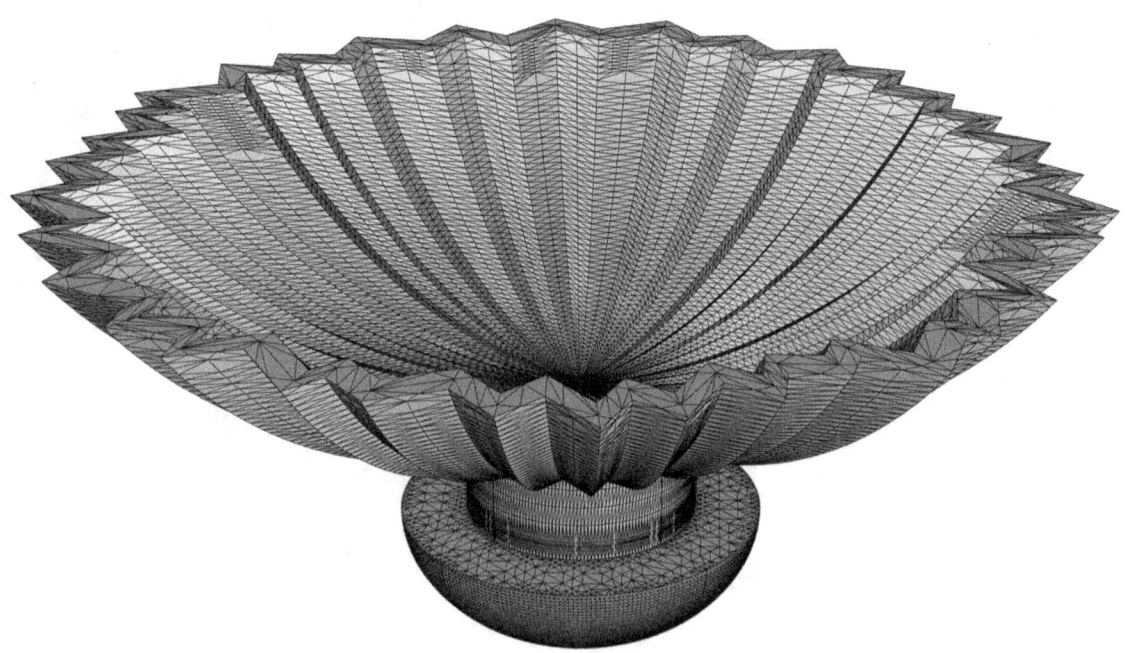

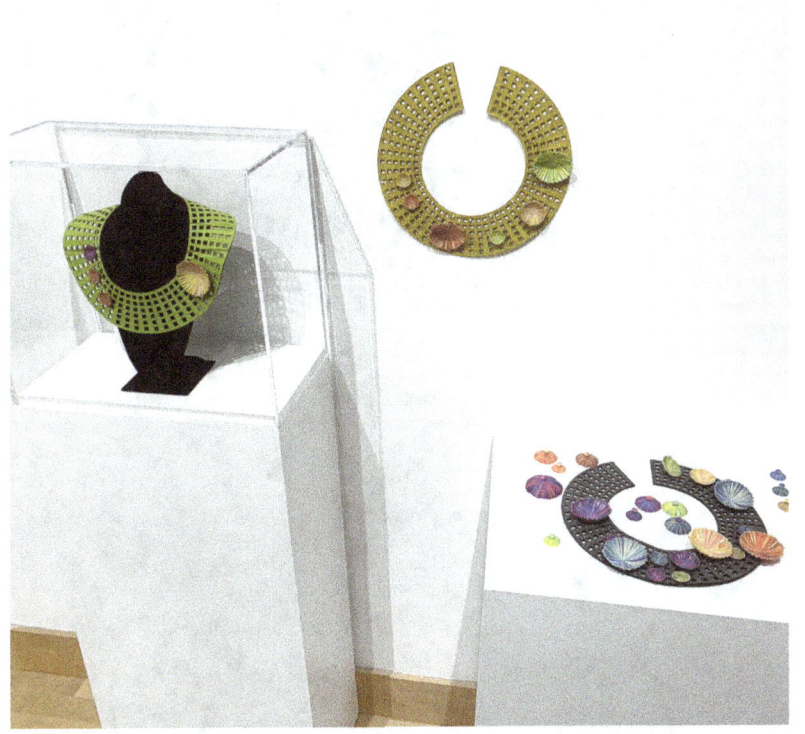

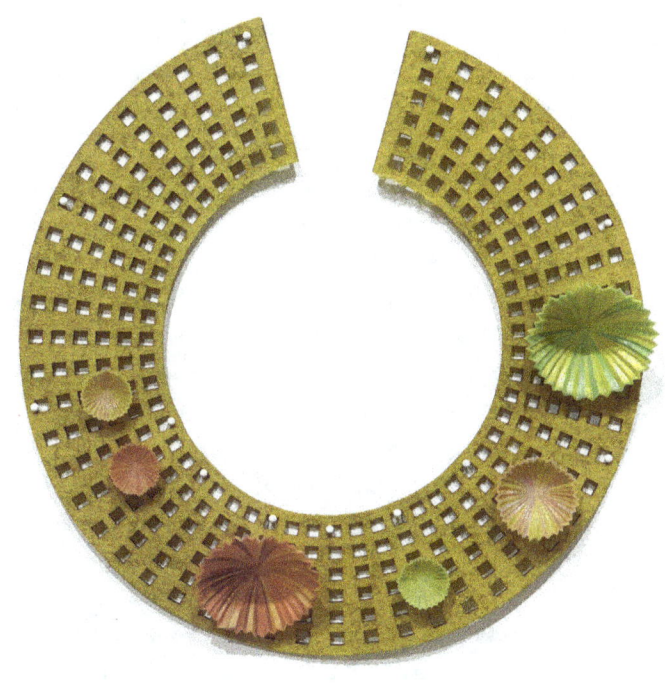

Maria Eife, *Lattice Garden,* 2019
Felt, gypsum, epoxy resin

BATHSHEBA GROSSMAN

Bathsheba Grossman is a sculptor using digital fabrication technology to create forms in 3-D printed steel and subsurface laser etching in glass. Her love of science, a sculptor's perfectionism, and CAD/CAM skills helped her transcend the limitations of traditional mold-making and casting techniques. She says, "I like to think about shapes. Sometimes I think of a new one. It's something I do without wanting very much to explain it." She often creates visual representations of complex structures such as proteins and molecules. Grossman's work has been exhibited in a variety of venues, including the Museum of Arts and Design, New York; MDI Biological Laboratory, Salisbury Cove, Maine; Velvet Da Vinci Gallery, San Francisco, California; East Stroudsburg University, Pennsylvania; and Southwestern University, Georgetown, Texas. Grossman is featured in *Digital Handmade, Craftsmanship in the New Industrial Revolution*; *3D Technology in Fine Art and Craft: Exploring 3D Printing, Scanning, Sculpting and Milling*; *Fabricated: The New World of 3-D Printing*; *Magazin Möbelmesse Köln*; *Symmetry* magazine; *Time* magazine; *The New York Times*; *WIRED*; and *American Craft* magazine. Her work has also appeared on the television shows CBS' Numb3rs and NBC's *Heroes*. Grossman works for *CrystalProteins*, a project she helped launch in 2002. *CrystalProteins* uses subsurface laser-etching technology to create visual representations of complex structures such as proteins, molecules, and other 3-D data in glass, for a range of uses, from research to decoration. She received her BA in Mathematics from Yale University and her MFA in Sculpture from the University of Pennsylvania.

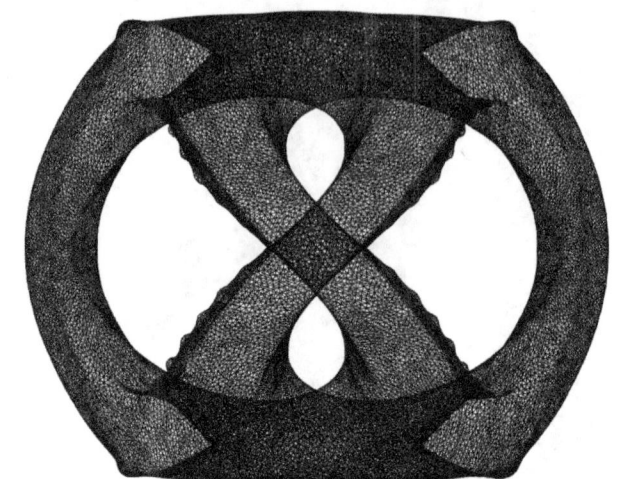

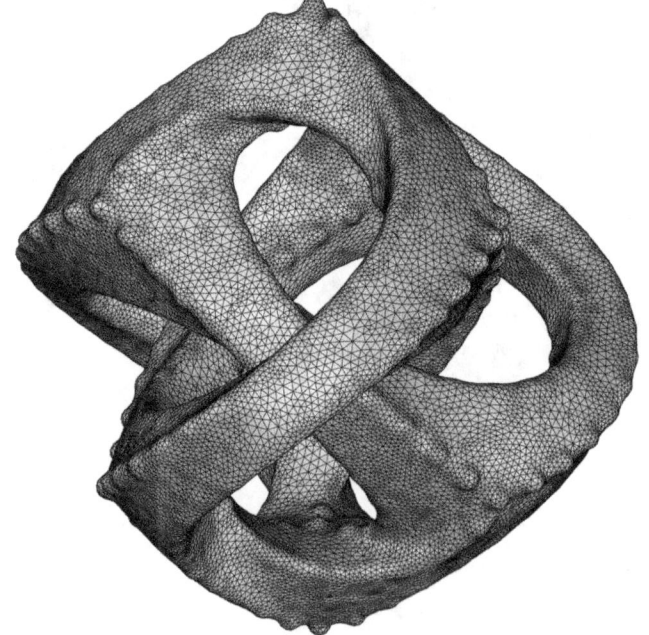

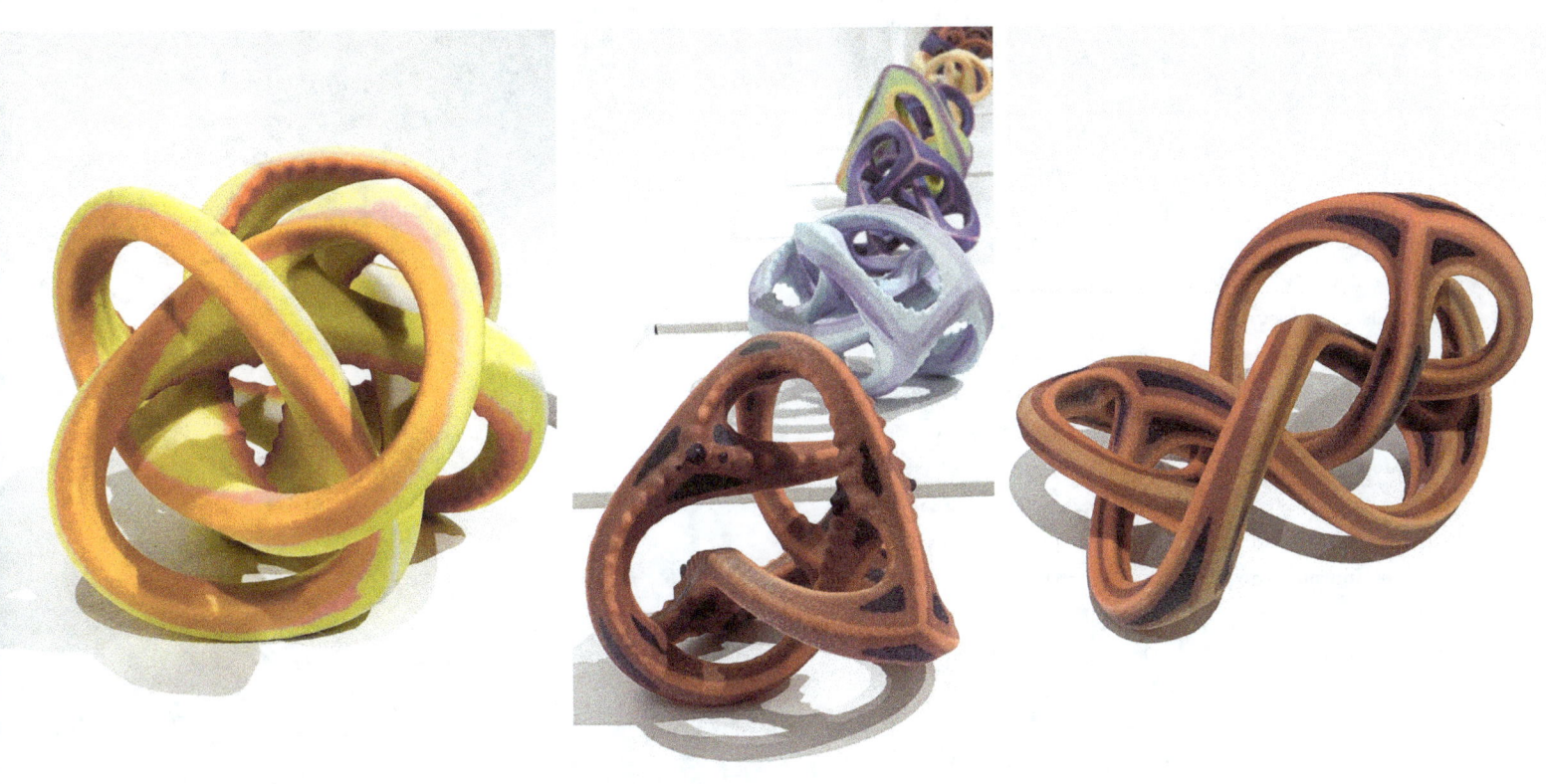

Bathsheba Grossman, *Zayana, Tritreda, Dovufo, Nunegi, Fatiku, Cujoyu, Jabobi, Tsedabu, Kiveva, Cebuca*, 2018
Gypsum, epoxy resin

DEL HARROW

Del Harrow is a sculptor and ceramicist creating work on the cutting edge of ceramic arts and technology. He utilizes a variety of traditional and contemporary processes, ranging from direct hand-building with clay coils and slabs to computer-aided design, parametric modelling, and computer-controlled machine fabrication. Harrow's work has been featured in many exhibitions: Foundation Bernardaud, Limoges, France; Center for Craft Creativity and Design, Asheville, North Carolina; Harvey Meadows Gallery, Aspen, Colorado; Museum of Fine Arts and the Society of Arts and Crafts, Boston, Massachusetts; Haw Contemporary, Kansas City, Missouri; Lilstreet Art Center, Chicago, Illinois; Milwaukee Art Museum, Wisconsin; Temple Contemporary, Tyler School of Art and Architecture, Philadelphia, Pennsylvania; Northern Clay Center, Minneapolis, Minnesota; The Denver Art Museum, Colorado; Arizona State University Art Museum, Tempe; Rowan University Art Gallery, Glassboro, New Jersey; the Urban Institute for Contemporary Art, Grand Rapids, Michigan; California College of Art, Oakland; and Montavallo State University, Alabama. His work is in the permanent collections of the US Embassy in Nuevo Laredo, Mexico and the Arizona State University Art Museum in Tempe. It has been featured in *Ceramics Art and Perception* and *500 Ceramic Sculptures* (Lark Books). He is the recipient of multiple awards and grants, including an NCECA Emerging Artist Award; a Faculty Research Grant, Institute for Arts and Humanities, Pennsylvania State University; and the Graham Foundation Grant, Chicago, Illinois. He has been an Artist-in-Residence at ART 342; The Archie Bray Foundation; and the Foshan/Nanfeng International Woodfire Conference in China. Harrow is currently an Associate Professor at Colorado State University, where he teaches sculpture, digital fabrication, and ceramics. He received his MFA from the New York State College of Ceramics at Alfred University, New York and his BS from the University of Oregon, Eugene. Harrow is represented by Haw Contemporary in Kansas City, Missouri and Harvey Meadows Gallery in Aspen, Colorado.

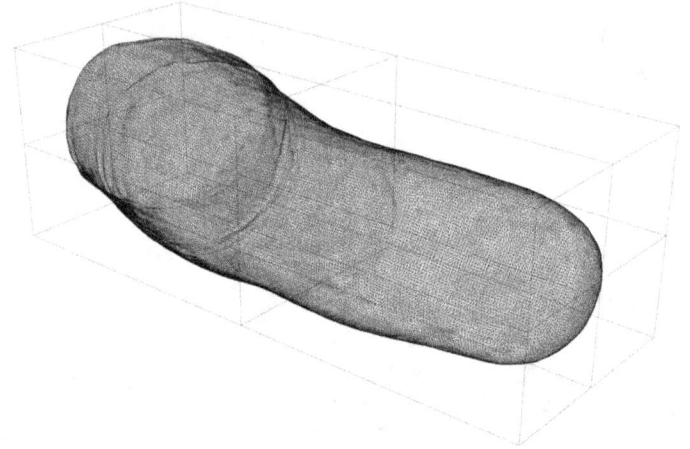

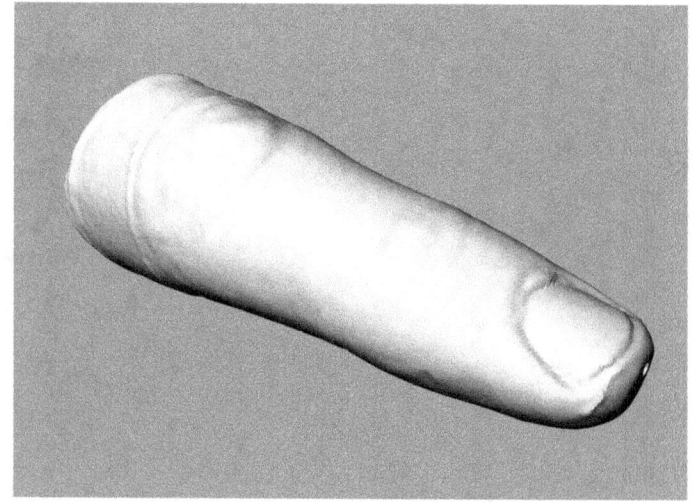

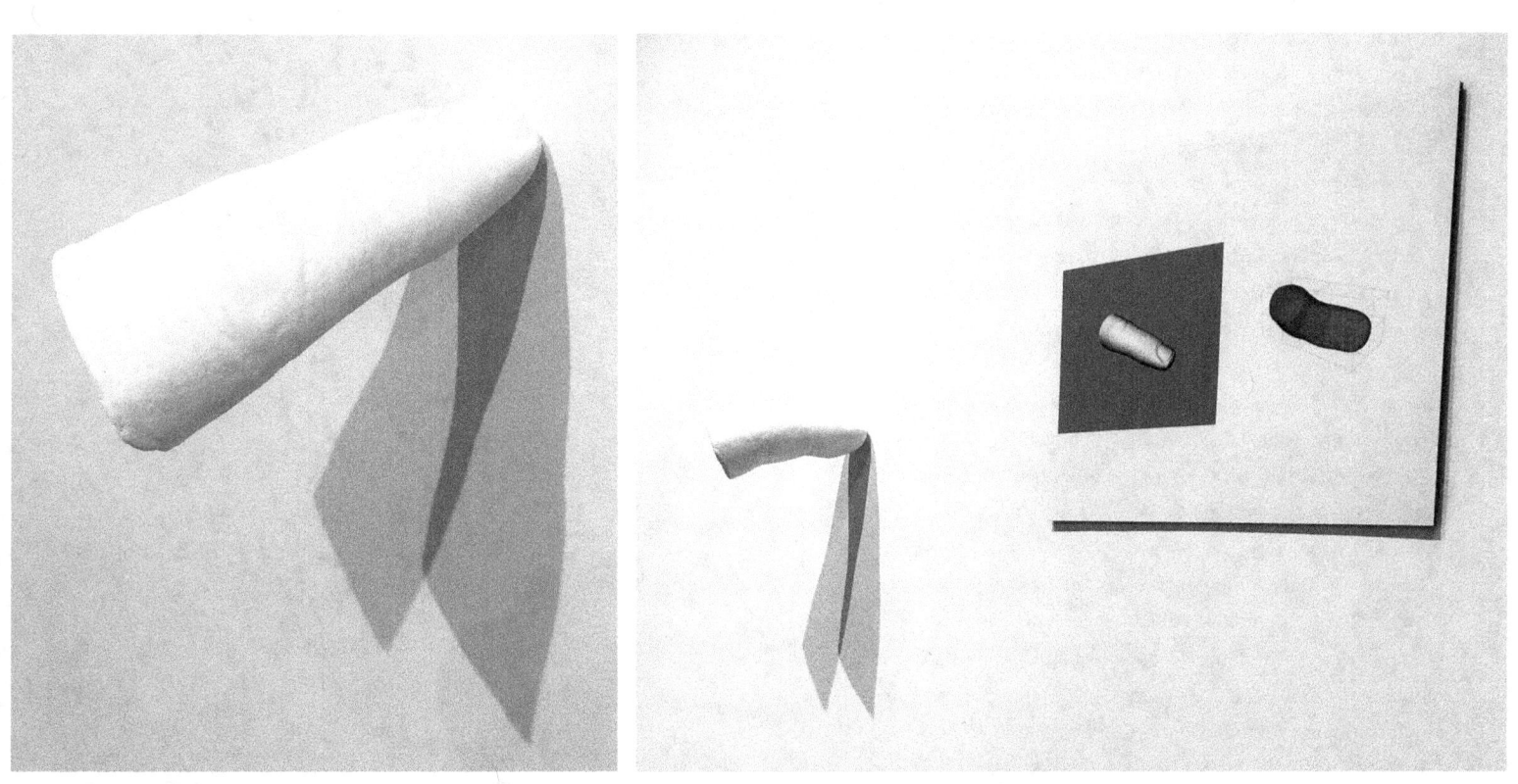

Del Harrow, *Touch*, 2018
Gypsum, epoxy resin

RYAN MANDELL

Ryan Mandell is a sculptor and furniture and product designer who creates forms meant to re-contextualize and re-evaluate architectural structures. Over time, he has incorporated digital fabrication technologies. Mandell comments, "The psychological state of a society, its tendencies, hopes, and fears, are illuminated by the structures it chooses to create, and the ways in which those structures are used... Repeated formal choices in architecture around the world betray a set of universal concerns and desires: modularity, order, efficiency, and convenience. The sculptural objects I create call into question the validity of adopting these characteristics as ideals." Mandell has exhibited nationally and internationally, with institutions such as Institute of Contemporary Art, Baltimore, Maryland; Grounds for Sculpture, Hamilton, New Jersey; John Michael Kohler Arts Center, Sheboygan, Wisconsin; Tuska Center for Contemporary Art, University of Kentucky, Lexington; SoFA Gallery, Indiana University, Bloomington; Hopkins Gallery, Ohio State University, Columbus; Redux Contemporary Art Center, Charleston, South Carolina; and Takt Kunstprojektraum and Praxislabor, both in Berlin, Germany. His work has also been featured in publications including *Sculpture Magazine*, and he has had reviews in both the *Baltimore City Paper* and the *Chicago Tribune*. Mandell has received awards and grants from the University of Wisconsin, Milwaukee; Indiana University, Bloomington; Milwaukee Institute of Art and Design, Wisconsin; Boise State University, Idaho; a Quick Funds Grant from the Idaho Commission on the Arts/National Endowment for the Arts, and an Outstanding Student Achievement in Contemporary Sculpture award from the International Sculpture Center/*Sculpture Magazine*. He received his BFA from the Milwaukee Institute of Art and Design, Wisconsin and his MFA in Sculpture from Indiana University, Bloomington. Mandell is the Director of Fabrication Labs at the Indiana University School of Art, Architecture + Design, Bloomington.

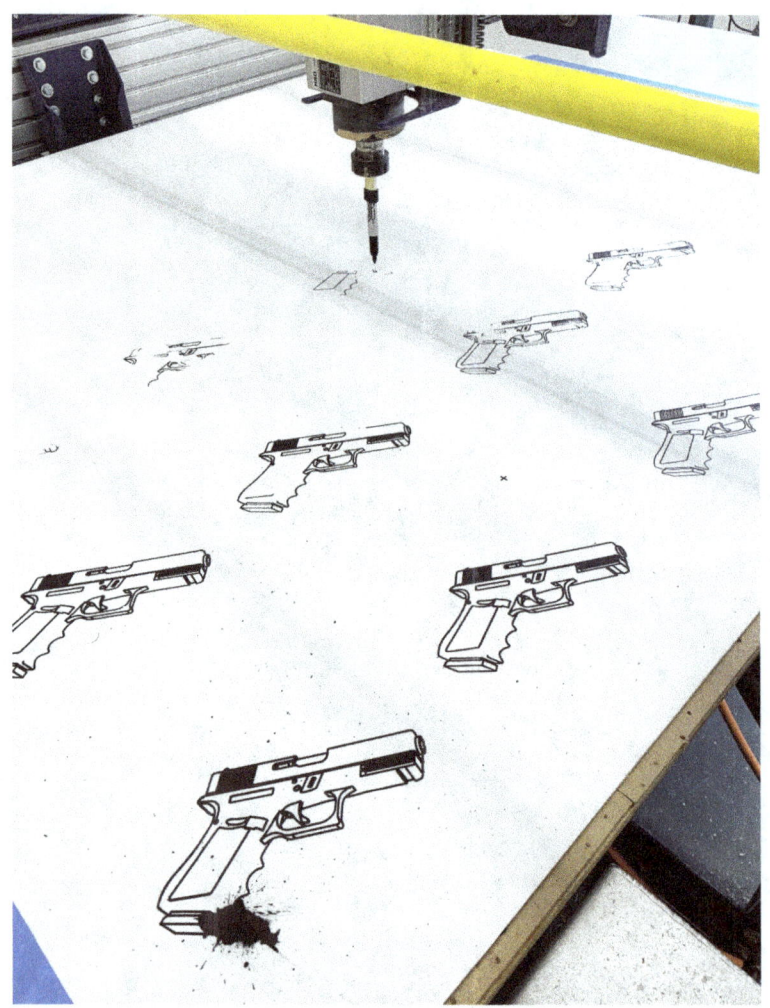

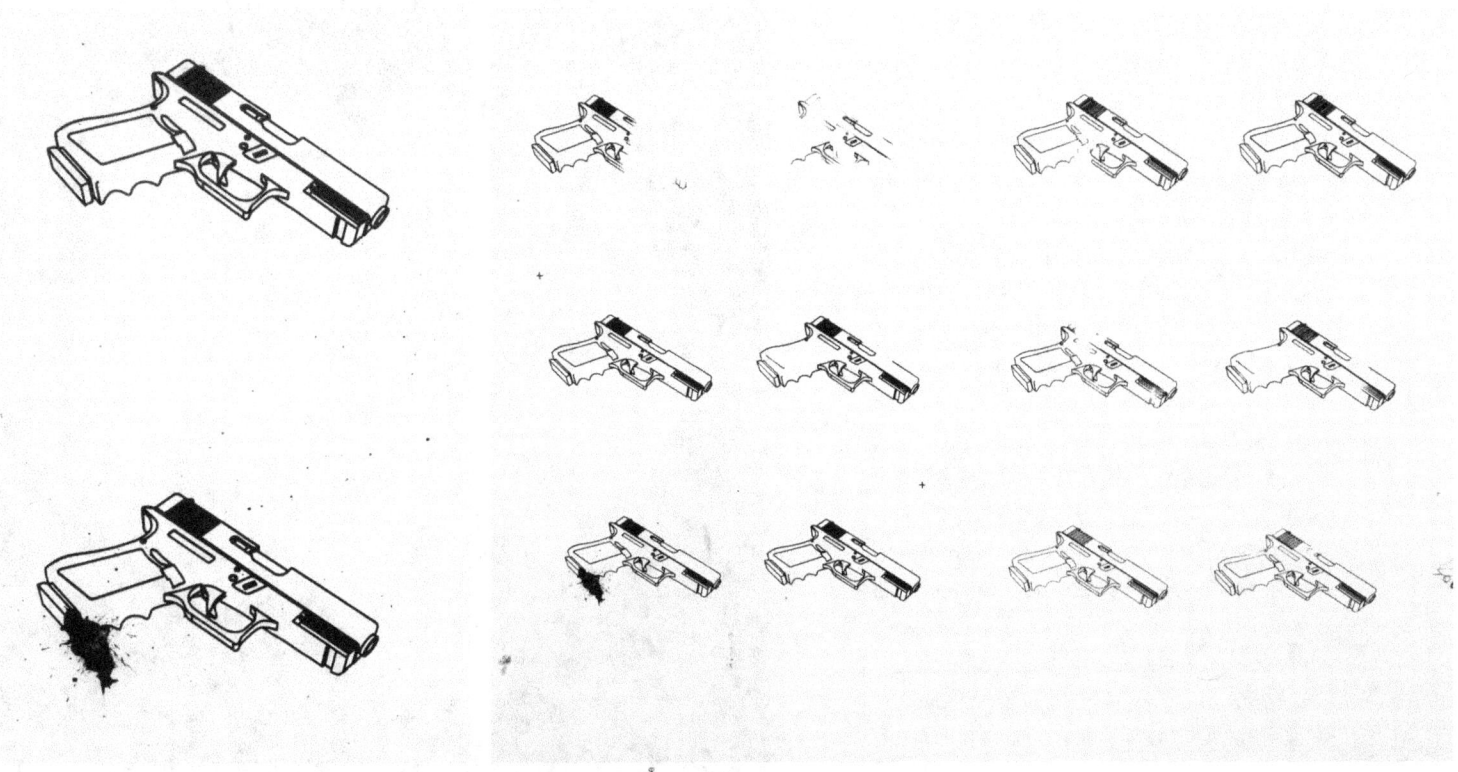

Ryan Mandell, *Glocks,* 2013
CNC plotted drawing on paper

Ryan Mandell, *Predators,* 2013
CNC plotted drawing on paper

JULIAN MAYOR

Julian Mayor is an East London-based designer and artist who combines industrial fabrication techniques with more traditional craft processes to create dynamic sculptural forms, furniture, architectural interventions, and objects. In an interview with *DesignBoom*, Mayor described his work as "techno-craft." He explains "'technology' is seen as a facilitator . . . a means to an end . . . craft." Mayor worked as a designer for prominent design studios including Pentagram before showing his own designs. His furniture, object design, and sculptural works have been featured in exhibitions and design events internationally, including the Pushkin Museum, Moscow, Russia; Design Museum Holon, Israel; Victoria and Albert Museum, London, England; Museum of Modern Art (MOMA), Museum of Art and Design, and 21st Gallery in Chelsea, all in New York; Museo Poldi Pezzoli, Milan, Italy; Design Miami Basel, Switzerland; Rossana Orlandi, Milan, Italy; and Tokyo Design Week, Japan. Mayor has shown his work internationally, including at Galerie Armel Soyer, Paris; and Interart Sculpture Park, near Eindhoven, the Netherlands. He also installed a permanent series of sculptural park benches behind the Tate Britain in Pimlico, London. His work has been featured in publications such as *500x Art in Public* and *Street Furniture* (Braun Publishing); *Telling Tales: Fantasy and Fear in Contemporary Design* (Victoria & Albert Museum), among many others. Mayor received his BA in Industrial Design from the University of Northumbria, Newcastle, England, and his MA from the Royal College of Art, London, England. He is represented by Galerie Armel Soyer in Paris, France; Rossana Orlandi, Milan, Italy; and 21st Gallery, New York.

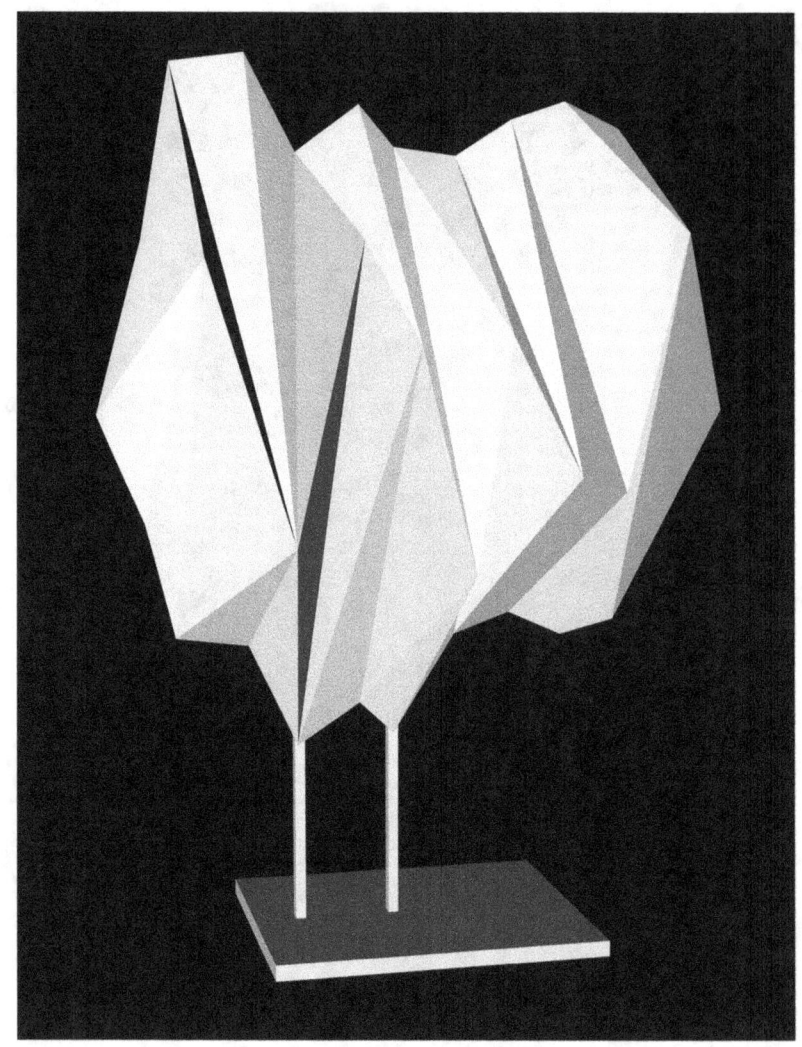

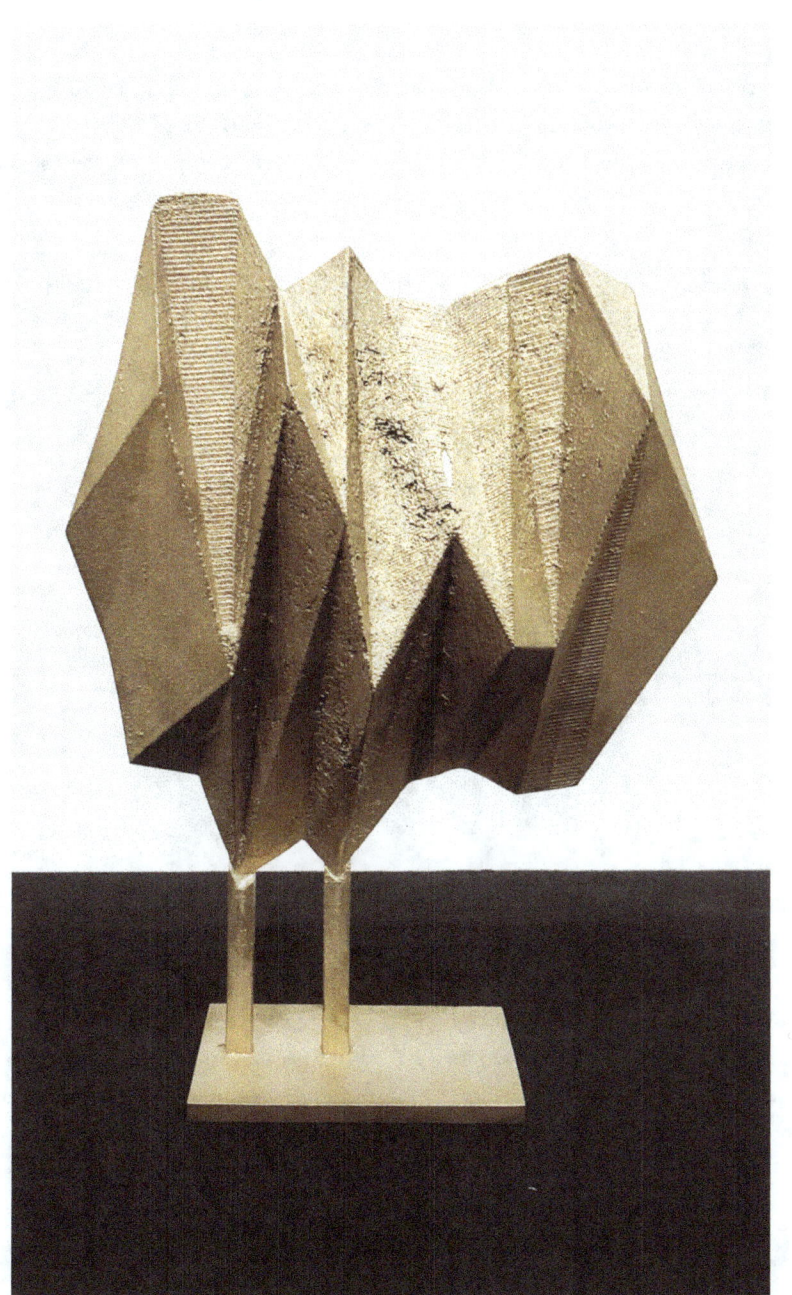

Julian Mayor, *Wing,* 2018
Cast bronze

ANNIKA PETTERSSON

Annika Pettersson was born in Karlskrona, Sweden. She works predominantly in the field of of contemporary jewelry by exploring traditional jewelry and reinterpretating classical shapes and forms. Her starting point is often an iconic theme, such as a brooch or necklace, which she investigates with different techniques and methods, resulting in distorted and deconstructed forms. She comments, "As a jewelry artist I am fascinated with value and authenticity, how these concepts are present in intimate objects." For Pettersson, the nature of jewelry is in its detail, technique, and direct

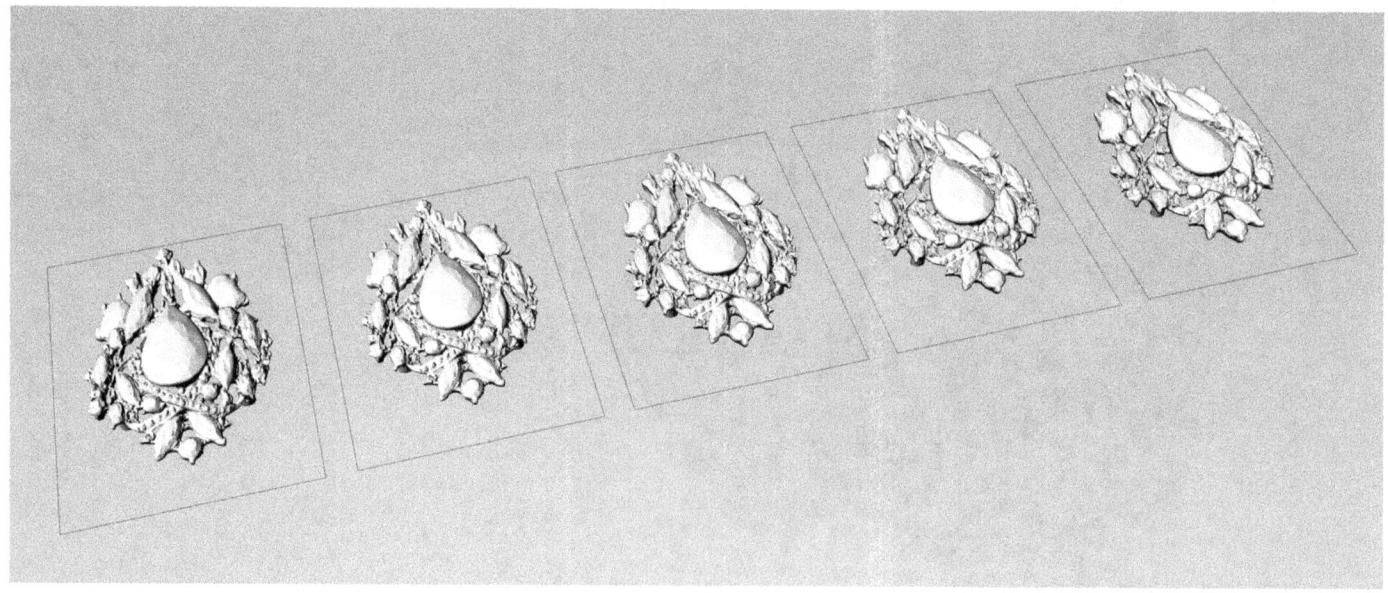

relationship to material. Her Remix project is based on the remix culture that emerged at the end of the 20th century, where artists (visual and musical among them) recombined pre-existing content. She finds that jewelry encompasses many ideas intrinsic to remixing's appropriated media format. Adding and removing elements is inherent to both remixing and traditional jewelry making. The result is a combination of the crafted with the digital and new modes of manufacture. Pettersson is a founding members of the group A5, an artistic collaborative focused on adornment, the body, and jewelry in cultural contexts. She finds that it is of great importance to have the two different sides in her practice; focused personal approach and experimental collaborations. She has participated in many national and international exhibitions, among them *21 Grams*, Art Hangzhou and *Triple Parade Biennial 2018*, How Art Museum, Shanghai, both in China; *Craft Council's 6th European Triennial of Contemporary Jewellery*, Mons, Belgium; and *Crafted: Objects in Flux*, Museum of Fine Arts, Boston, Massachusetts. Pettersson has been awarded several prestigious grants. She has a BFA and MFA from Konstfack University, Stockhom, Sweden. She currently lives and works in Stockholm.

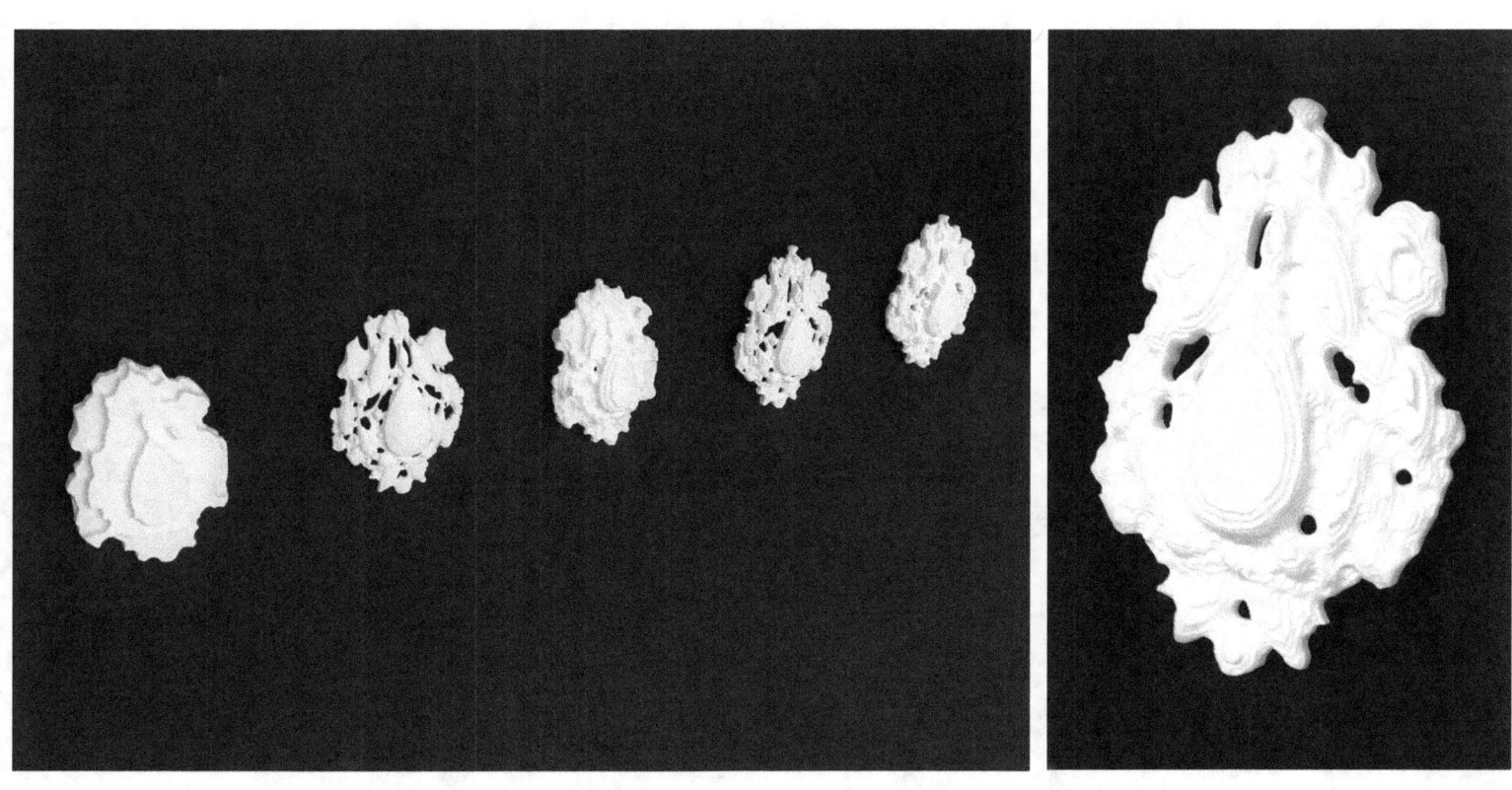

Annika Pettersson, *Remix Resolution,* 2018
Corian

PHIL RENATO

Phillip Renato is a third-generation metalworker from a family of millwrights who built and maintained automotive assembly lines and nuclear power plants. Renato points out that he has spent his career "designing and producing mostly one-of-a-kind objects of significantly less practical value [and not necessarily in metal.]" He designs and constructs objects that are jewelry and product-adjacent, and "crafts dreams," making things that have not yet existed and that no one needs, but that reflect his values. His creations are simultaneously innovative and beautiful and employ contemporary processes and materials; he thinks of himself as a "poet of post-products." Renato has shown his work in over 50 exhibitions, including Lillstreet Arts Center in Chicago, Illinois; Shemer Center for the Arts, Phoenix, Arizona; the Alden B. Dow Museum of Science and Art, Midland, Michigan; and the Urban Institute for Contemporary Art, Grand Rapids, Michigan. His writing and artwork have appeared on the cover of *Metalsmith* magazine and in the pages of numerous other periodicals and books, among them the series of Lark books: *500 Necklaces, 500 Wedding Rings, The Art of Plastic Jewelry*, and *500 Knives*. He presents workshops on CAD modeling and the use of plastics for jewelry production, as well as lectures on his work and collaborates on projects across the United States and internationally including Portugal, China, and the United Arab Emirates. His art is in the collection of the Spertus Institute for Jewish Learning and Leadership, Chicago, Illinois, among others. Renato holds an MFA in Metal Design from the University of Washington, Seattle and a BFA in Metalsmithing, Painting, and Creative Writing from Eastern Michigan University. He is a Professor and Chair of the Metals/Jewelry and Industrial Design, Allesee MJD Program, Kendall College of Art and Design, Grand Rapids, Michigan, a program which he founded.

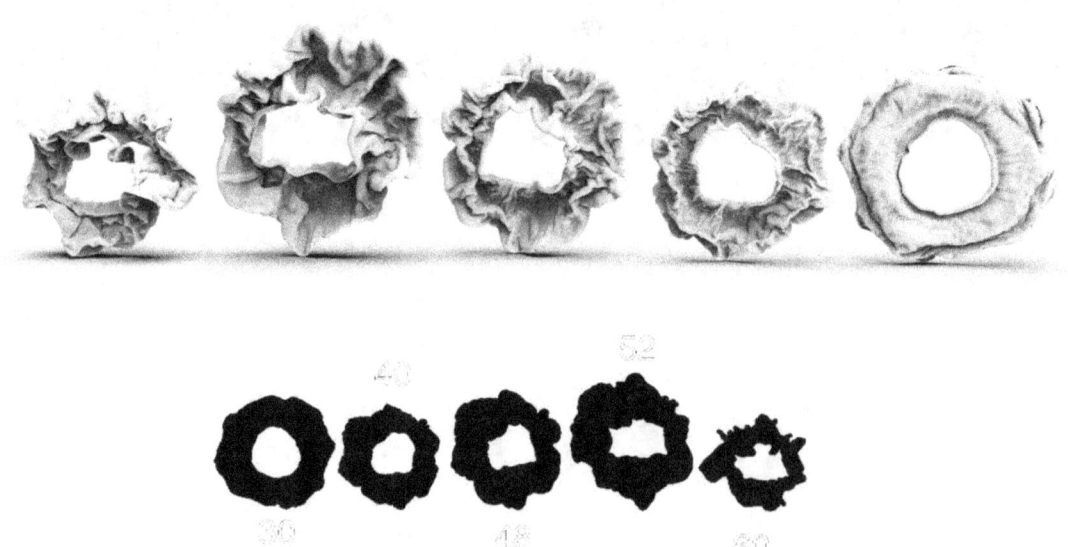

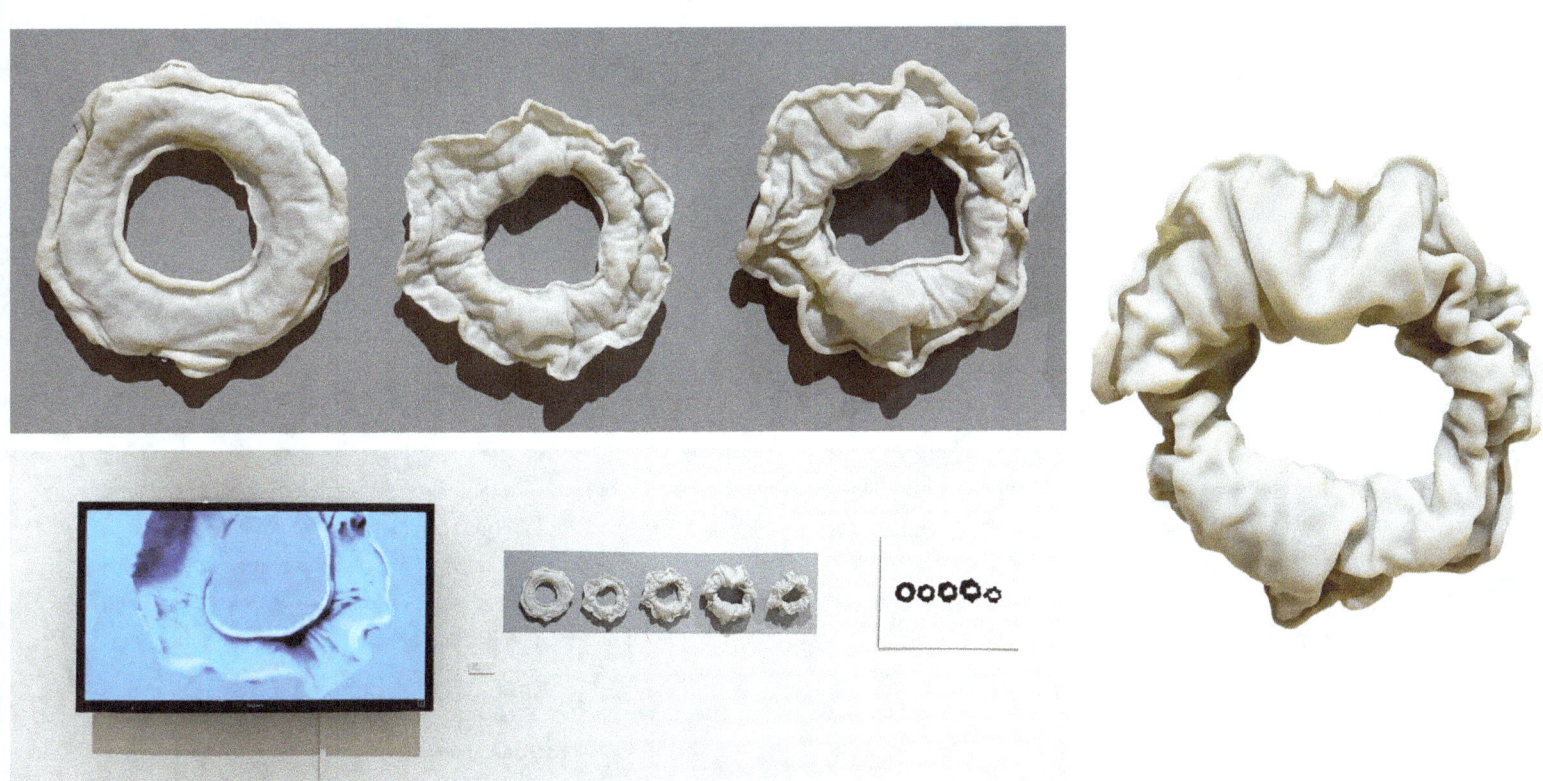

Phil Renato, *Palillogia*, 2018
Photopolymer

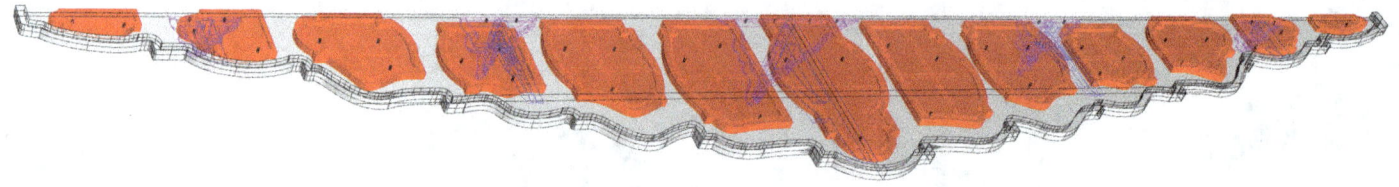

J. ALEX SCHECHTER

J. Alex Schechter describes himself as a multimedia sculptor. He arrives at the shapes of objects through a process that asks what can be done with digital fabrication that would be difficult or impossible to do with traditional craft methodology? In his sculpture for *Form.Print*, he wanted to represent, or map, or reflect, a space that can never be viewed. Working from an open source database of CT scans, he used a variety of software to create physical manifestations of the interior spaces of skulls. He comments that, "when printed, the resulting objects are both familiar and uncanny, pointing towards the unseen abstractions that silently dictate both the natural and built world." He has shown his work in the Sykes Gallery, Millersville University and Vox Populi, Philadelphia, both in Pennsylvania; the University of Cumbria, United Kingdom; Flux Factory and Sculpture Space, both in New York (where he was an Artist-in-Residence); Terrault Contemporary, Baltimore, Maryland; Ten Gallery, Purple Walls Gallery, and Good Children Gallery, all in New Orleans, Louisiana; The Owl's Nest, Seattle, Washington; and FOMMA Trust, Karachi, Pakistan, among others. Schechter holds an MFA in Sculpture from the Rinehart School of Sculpture, Maryland Institute College of Art, Baltimore; a BA in Studio Art and Religious Studies from Grinnell College, Iowa; and Certification in Post-Secondary Arts Education from MICA. He is adjunct faculty at the Tyler School of Art and Architecture at Temple University, Philadelphia, Pennsylvania; Towson University; and Rowan University, New Jersey.

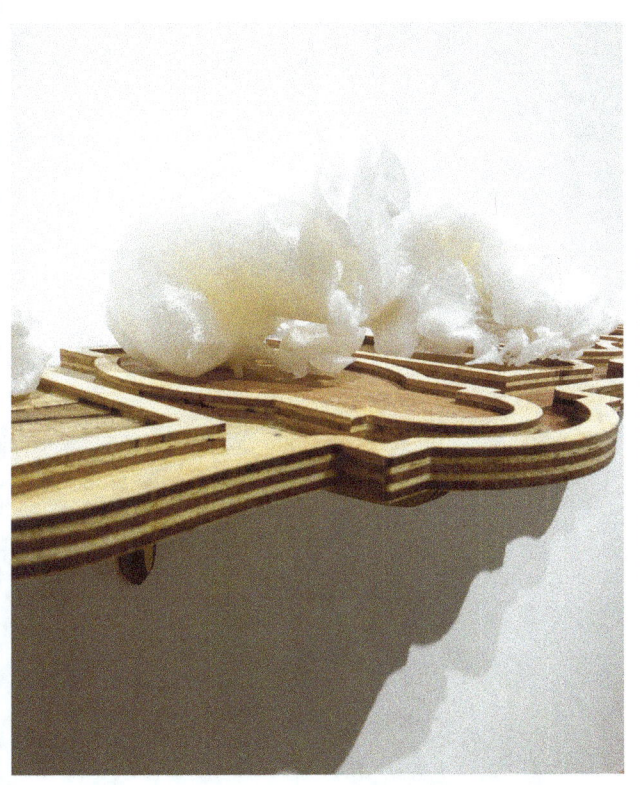

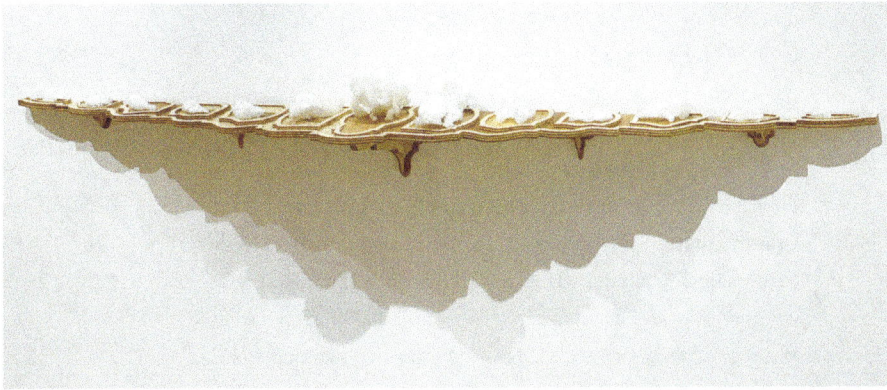

Alex Schecter, *Evidence Such As This,* 2018
PLA, Plywood

ERIC STANDLEY

Eric Standley is known for his remarkably detailed laser-cut paper artworks created at the nexus of technology, mythology, and geometry. He states, "Drawing is at the core of my studio practice. Organizing objects in space begins on a 2-D plane in my sketch books and is further elaborated on as vectors in CorelDraw." Each layer, or "event," is cut, then stacked into the completed artwork. He does not use processing or algorithm-generated elements but instead draws each line individually, keeping in mind a holistic goal. His technology-infused studio practice enables him to create complex artifacts within a realm of precision that is often reserved for industry, mass production, and scientific research. *The Lesson of Atticus*, his contribution to *Form. Print*, is made from Kometex (foamed PVC sheets). Standley believes that visual archetypes can trigger sight-meditation which aligns thought, pattern, and presence. He is currently working with scientists investigating chromatin architecture and the fractal geometry of DNA. From this investigation, he seeks visual archetypes from the most profoundly universal building blocks of life. His works have been exhibited in over 120 galleries and museums around the world and are a part of many national and international collections including the Palace of Sharjah, United Arab Emirates; the Scherenschnitt Museum, Vreden, Germany; and the Zupi Collection of São Paulo, Brazil. Standley has been featured on the Discovery Channel of Canada; Luxe TV, Luxembourg; and Mezamashi National TV of Japan. He lives and works in Blacksburg, Virginia. Standley received his BFA from the Massachusetts College of Art and his MFA from the Savannah College of Art and Design. He is an Associate Professor at Virginia Tech, where he teaches principles of art and design as well as CNC laser fabrication techniques. Standley is represented by Victori + Mo, New York City; the Marta Hewett Gallery, Cincinnati, Ohio; and Media Force, Tokyo, Japan.

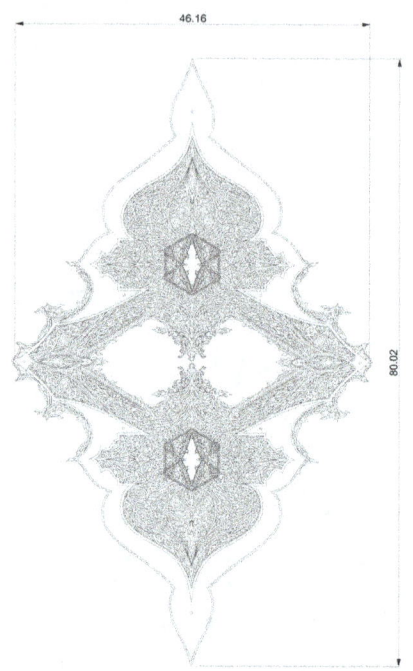

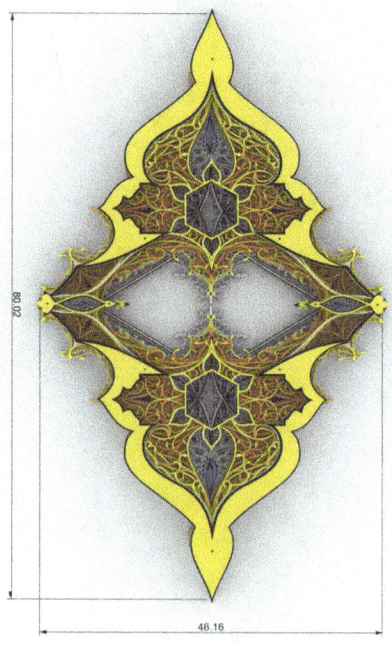

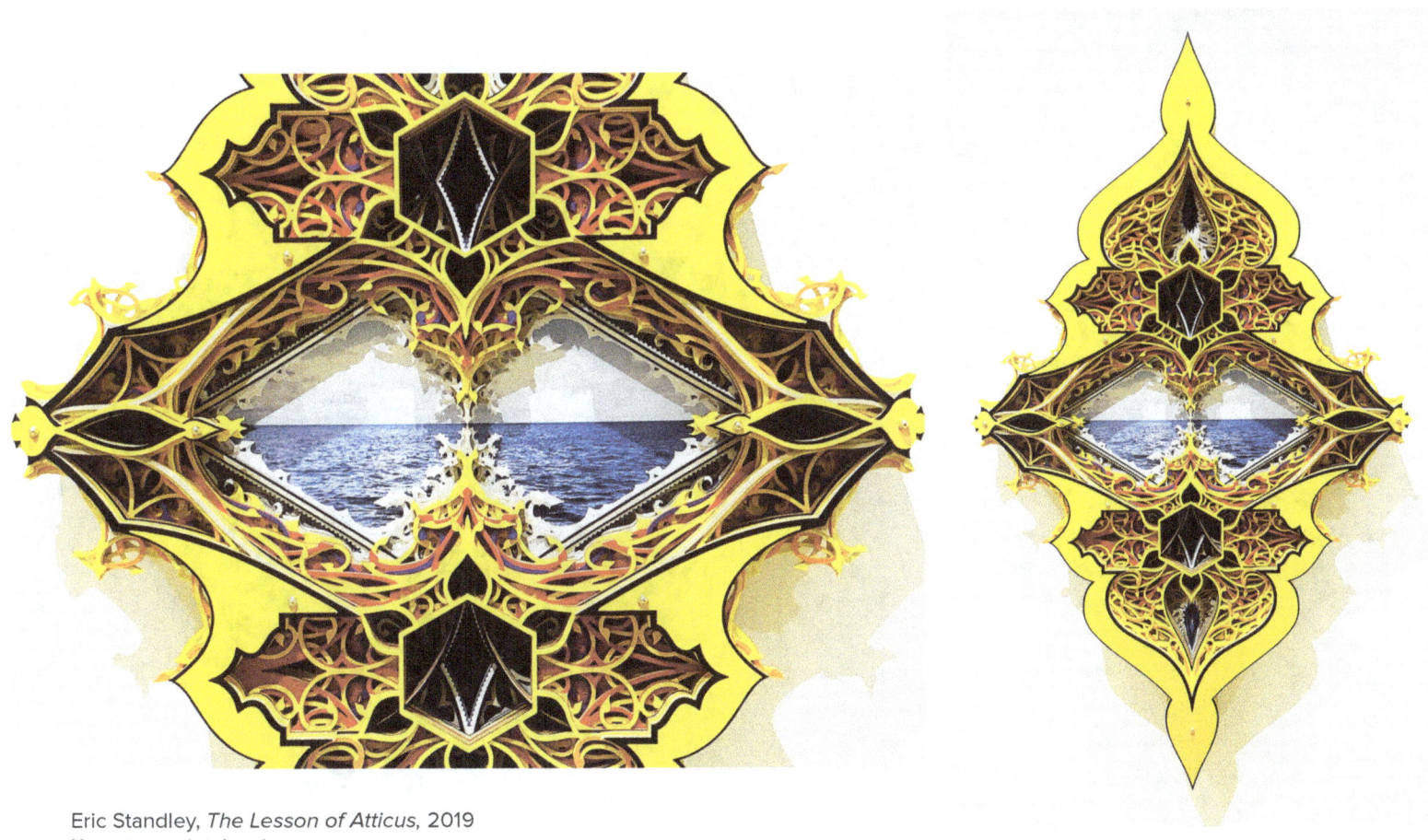

Eric Standley, *The Lesson of Atticus,* 2019
Kometex, print, hardware

CHRIS BOYD TAYLOR

Chris Boyd Taylor is a sculptor concerned with utilizing craft, scale, color, and movement to create forms that reference and simulate architecture, memory, spectatorship, imagination, anthropomorphism, and interpersonal relationships. He notes: "The work I create comes from a fascination with the transformative power of the places where we reside and the memories and imagination they elicit... I imagine: what would it be like to be there?" Taylor's work invites the viewer to reminisce with him. It has been included and on view in numerous exhibitions and projects, including at the Bethea Gallery, School of Design, Louisiana Tech University, Ruston; Circle Gallery, College of Environment + Design, University of Georgia, Athens; Coop Gallery, Nashville, Tennessee; the Montgomery Museum of Fine Art; Abroms-Engel Institute for the Arts, Birmingham; Huntsville Museum of Art, and the Lowe Mill ARTS & Entertainment, Huntsville, all in Alabama; the Columbus College of Art & Design, Ohio; Socrates Sculpture Park, Long Island City; The Belfry, Hornell; Cohen Center for the Arts, Alfred; Wellsville Art Center; and The Miller Theatre, Alfred, all in New York. He also has had public artworks on display at Nashville International Airport, Tennessee; Austin Peay State University, Clarksville, Tennessee; and Pablo Neruda Plaza, Montevideo, Uruguay. Taylor has received several awards, grants, and fellowships, including the McMahon-Pleiad Prize for the Collaborative Public Art Trail, the University of Alabama System, Tuscaloosa; a New Faculty Research Grant from the University of Alabama, Huntsville; and Socrates Sculpture Park, New York. He has been featured and received reviews in *The New York Times*; *Nashville Scene*; *Number: Inc*; and *Brooklyn Based*. Taylor received his BFA in Sculpture from Ohio State University, Columbus and his MFA in Sculpture and Dimensional Studies from New York State College of Ceramics at Alfred University, New York. He is an Assistant Professor of Sculpture at the University of Alabama in Huntsville.

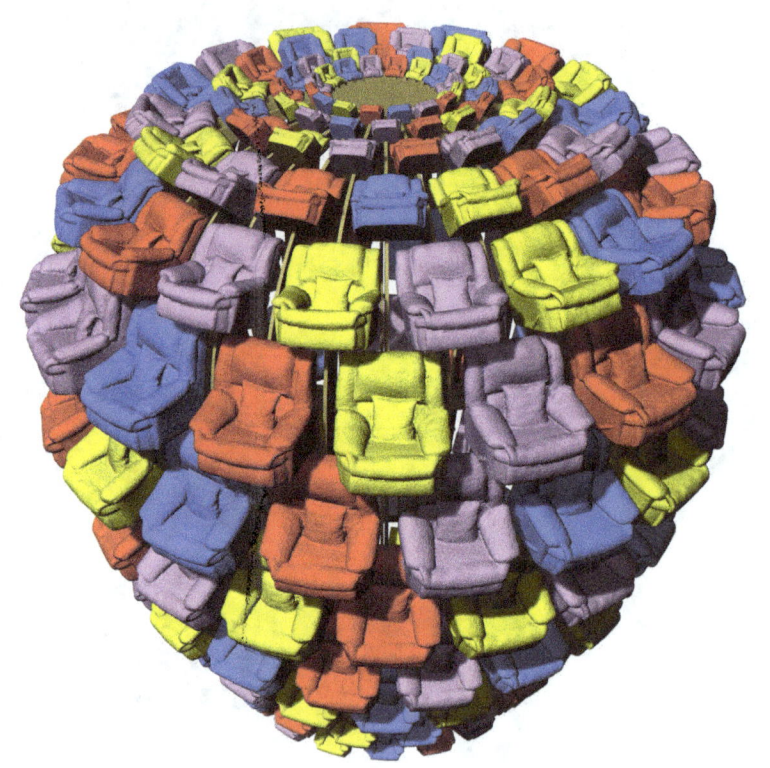

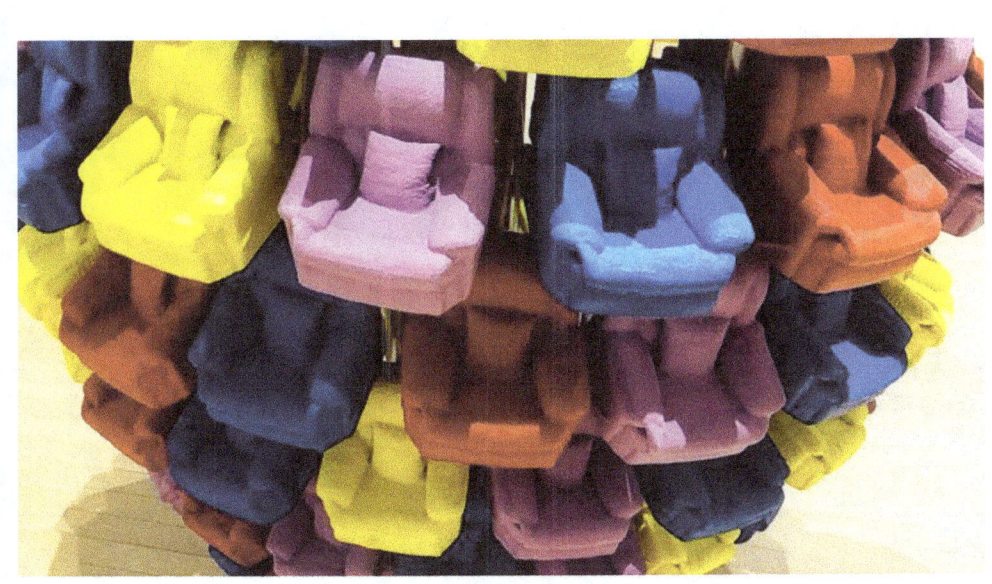

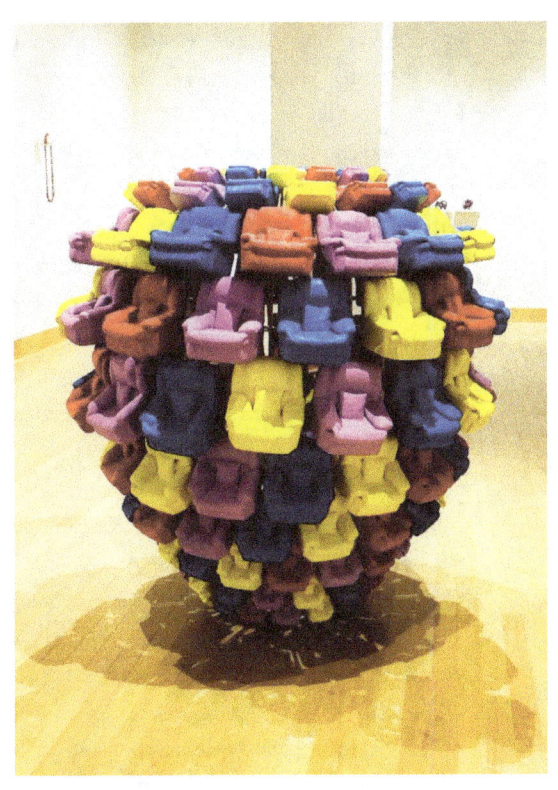

Chris Boyd Taylor, *Armchair Vase,* 2018
PLA, Plywood

KATJA TOPORSKI

Katja Toporski grew up in Germany where she nearly apprenticed to become a goldsmith, but instead attended medical school in Hamburg and Munich. She specialized in anesthesiology, ultimately practicing in the United Kingdom, and is a Fellow of the Royal College of Anaesthetists. While in the UK, she completed a City and Guilds certificate in Fine Jewelry as a way to decompress from the stress of her job. Upon her move to the United States, she became a full-time jeweler. She comments, "Having been a practicing anesthesiologist in the past, my work is informed by philosophical thinking, and juxtaposes archetypal objects and materials to explore the limitations of our understanding of things. I aim to navigate the various roles of jewelry and explore its spiritual and amuletic nature in the forms I apply... While perhaps not immediately obvious, to my mind there are certain questions at the core of the human condition that both art and medicine have to confront." Her work has been shown in numerous exhibitions, both in the US and Europe. It has been highlighted online in *Shifting Sites: Exhibition in Print* by *Metalsmith*. It has been on view in the Radierverein Gallery, Munich, Germany; Ombré Gallery, Cincinnati, Ohio; Geofrey A. Wolpert Gallery, Arrowmont School of Arts and Crafts, Gatlinburg, Tennessee; Alliages, Lille, France; The Permanent Gallery, Vilnius, Lithuania; Baltimore Jewelry Center and Maryland Art Place, both in Maryland; Special Collections Library, University of Milwaukee, Michigan; Santa Monica Arts, Barcelona, Spain; Adorned Spaces, Boston, Massachusetts; Brooklyn Metal Works, New York; Soo Visual Art Center, Minneapolis, Minnesota; Heidi Lowe Gallery, Rehoboth Beach, Delaware; and Jewelerswerk Gallery, Washington D.C. She has been honored with awards, including by the Italian Association for Contemporary Jewelry and the Society of North American Goldsmiths (SNAG). Toporski holds an MFA in Studio Art (Metals and Jewelry), from Towson University, and a Certificate in Fine Jewelry from City & Guilds, Portsmouth, as well as a Medical Degree from the Technical University, Munich, Germany. She teaches in the Washington, D.C. region.

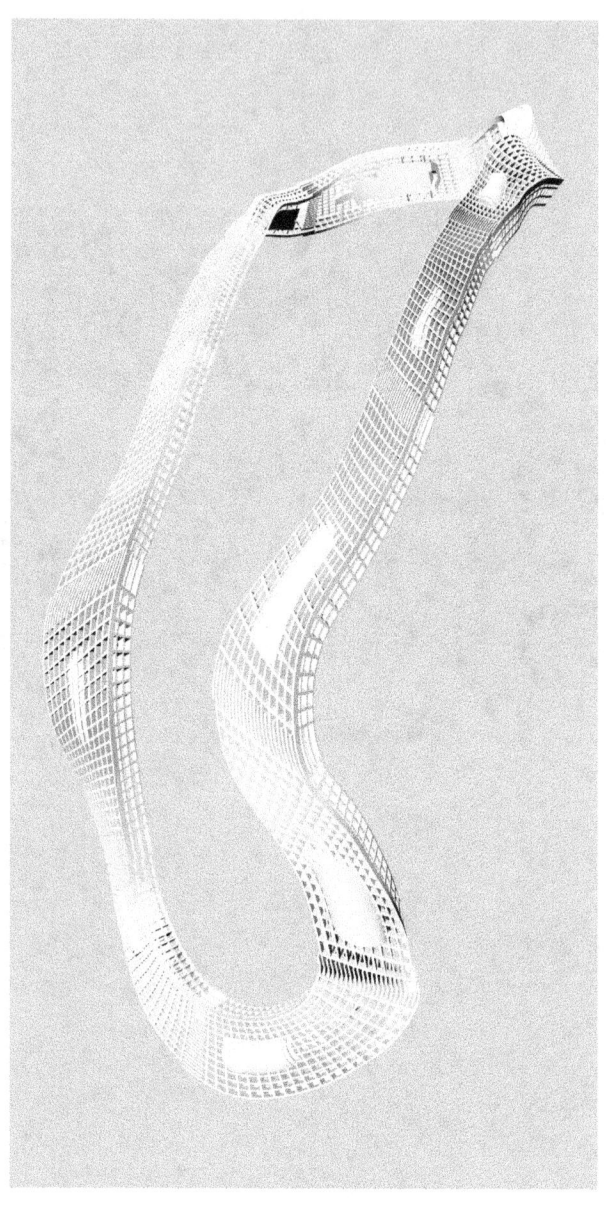

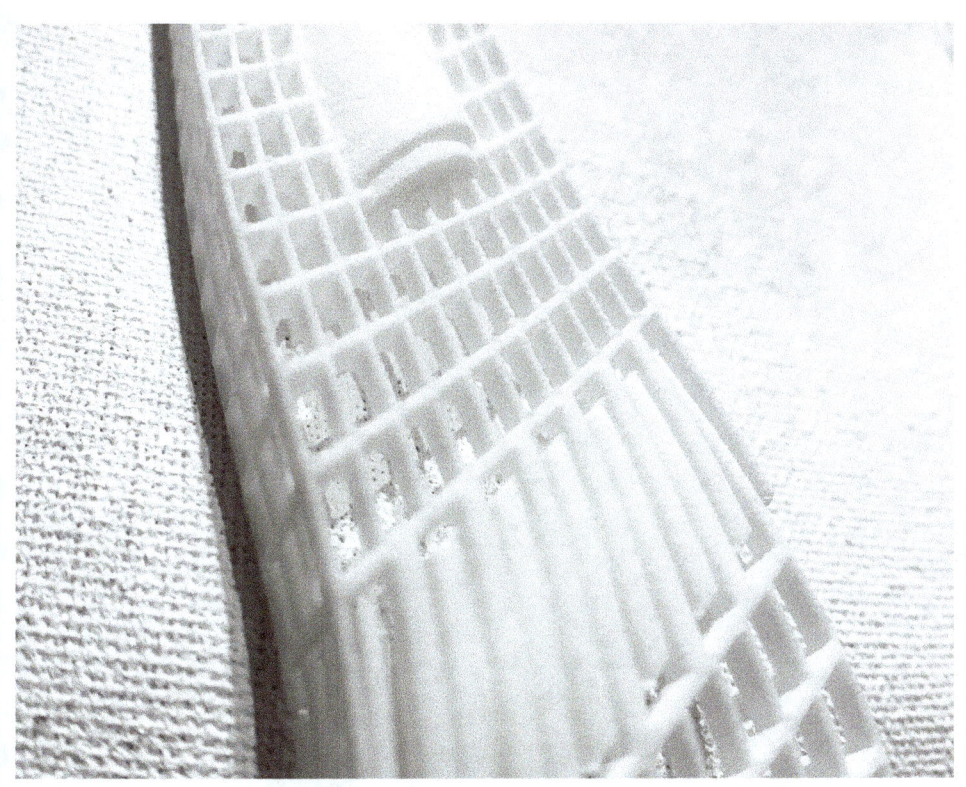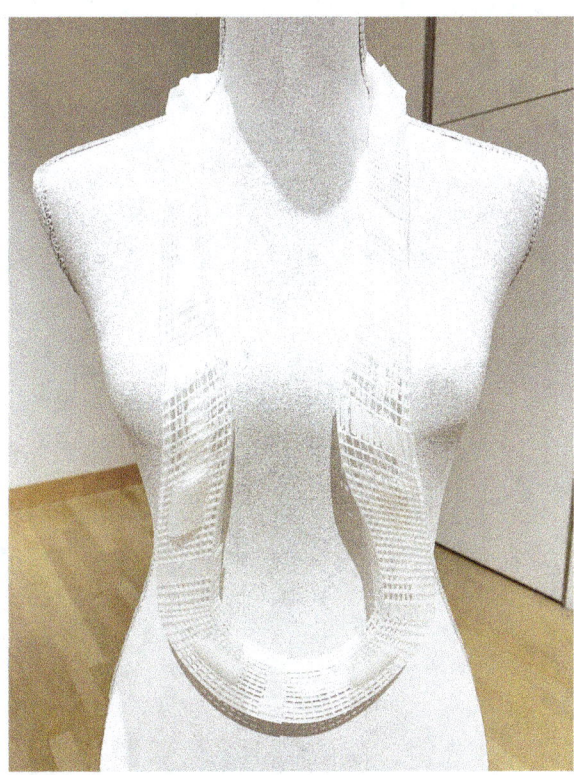

Katja Toporski, *Flask,* 2019
Nylon

COLIN WIENCEK

Colin Wiencek is a designer and maker who combines digital and traditional fabrication to create innovative furniture, lighting, architecture, and multimedia designs. He states: "C.Wiencek Design is a product design studio specializing in furniture and home goods. We are jointly focused on design licensing and the manufacture and sale of an in-house brand of luxury furnishings." What captivates him about furniture and object design is the ability of an object to affect social interaction. He explains: "By playing with proximity and dimension I am able to suggest certain types of interactions between people." He exhibited his first collection of furniture and lighting as a freelance designer at the *Wanted Design LaunchPad* exhibition hosted by *NYCxDesign*, New York. Among the works in his collection were a line of LED light fixtures that utilize modular construction and digitally fabricated components to create visually intricate geometric forms with minimal complexity of fabrication. Wiencek was awarded an Artist-in-Residence Fellowship in Furniture Design at the Anderson Ranch Art Center in Aspen, Colorado. He has also been a recipient of a Sustainability in Design Award from the Department of Furniture Design at Rhode Island School of Design. He received his BFA in Furniture Design with an additional concentration in History, Philosophy + Social Science from the Rhode Island School of Design in Providence. He is currently based in Washington, D.C. where he works as a freelance designer.

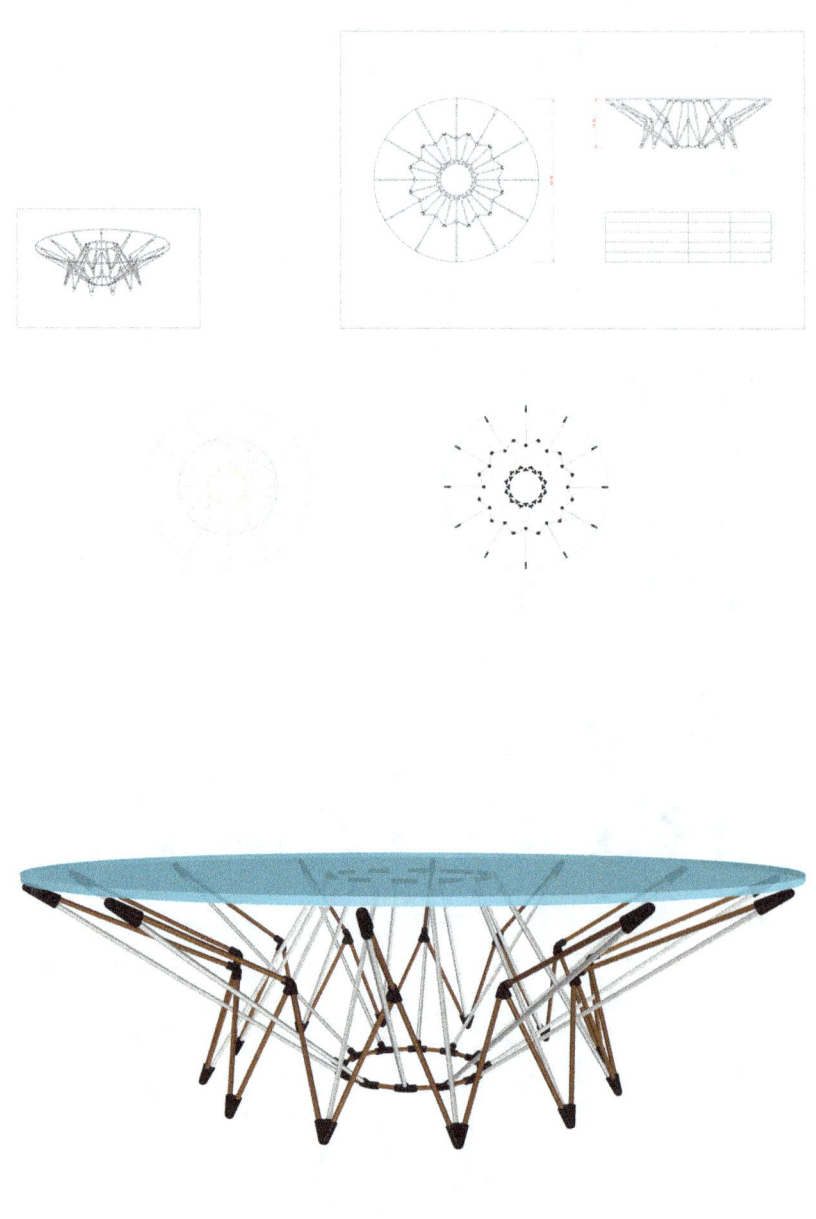

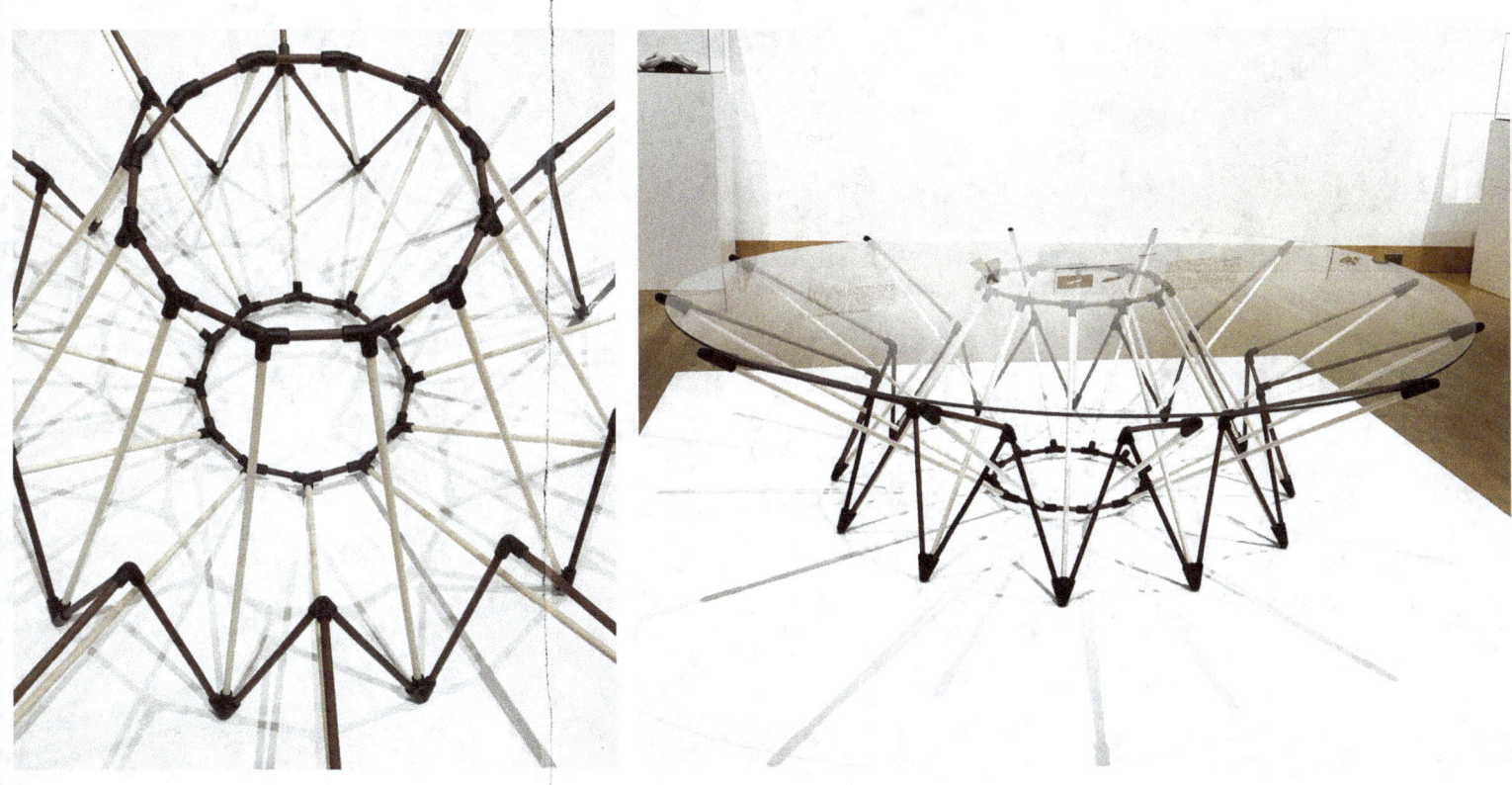

Colin Wiencek, *Circle Table,* 2018
Black printed resin hubs, bleached walnut dowels,
walnut dowels, Plexiglass top

form.print : A STUDENT PERSPECTIVE

Since *Form.Print* highlighted artists who use digital fabrication procedures in their practice, they sent digital files rather than finished artwork. Students and faculty in the Interdisciplinary Object Design and Sculpture programs printed the work using the technologies available at Towson University. During the Fall 2018 semester, Professor and guest curator Joshua DeMonte had students in the upper digital object design course prepare files for the exhibition and offered us an opportunity to work through the winter semester as interns to assist in the fabrication and installation process. Throughout the internship, Professor DeMonte provided a task list for the week. He worked around our schedules in order to have things completed each Friday.

The work in the exhibition presented several unique challenges. The base for Chris Boyd Taylor's *Armchair Vase*, for example, includes 32 wooden pieces cut using the Shopbot in the sculpture studio, along with 192 plastic armchairs that we printed using the Makerbot and Ultimaker printers on campus. Due to the variety of plastic filament used in the printers, each chair had to be primed and painted the specific color after printing but before being glued into place on the wooden base. The biggest issue when printing the chairs was the wait time. While we could print all of the smaller sizes at once, we had to print the larger sizes one at a time. It could take up to eight hours to print a single chair. This meant that throughout the process we had to keep a checklist of elements already printed, those left to print, those already primed, and those chairs already glued in place on the wooden frame. Having this system certainly helped, but it also meant that there were days we only painted half a dozen chairs because of the slow print time.

Another work that required multiple processes was *Inheritance* by Annet Couwenberg. Students used the Shopbot in the sculpture studio to cut the 54 stacking pieces that made up the base, as well as the top, which were then removed from the larger sheet of plywood, filed, sanded, and assembled using small wooden dowels. Once everything was in order, they were glued together, sanded again, and finally painted. Even though the base is hollow, it took a team of four to assemble and move the work due to its size. In the object lab, the small canopies for the face were printed and infiltrated before placing them on the milled work. The top, where these canopies now sat, was the most difficult part to construct since it had to be milled and sanded, and then any gaps or chips in the plywood filled with wood putty to ensure a correct fit before being painted.

The opportunity for students to collaborate with each other and with faculty, as well as make work with the artists, was incredibly rewarding. Being able to take the files sent to us and prepare a plan for fabrication, completion, finishing, and installation allowed for a better idea of how intense this process can be. Students involved in the fabrication also got the chance to work with new materials and more complex Shopbot procedures than those typically utilized in coursework. Working with both IOD and the Department of Art + Design Galleries staff was extremely beneficial in learning firsthand just how complicated preparing and planning for an exhibition can be. In the end, we hoped that this exhibition would encourage students and visitors to learn more about the role of 3-D printing and digital fabrication practices in the art field and incorporate them in their own projects.

Kayla Boyer

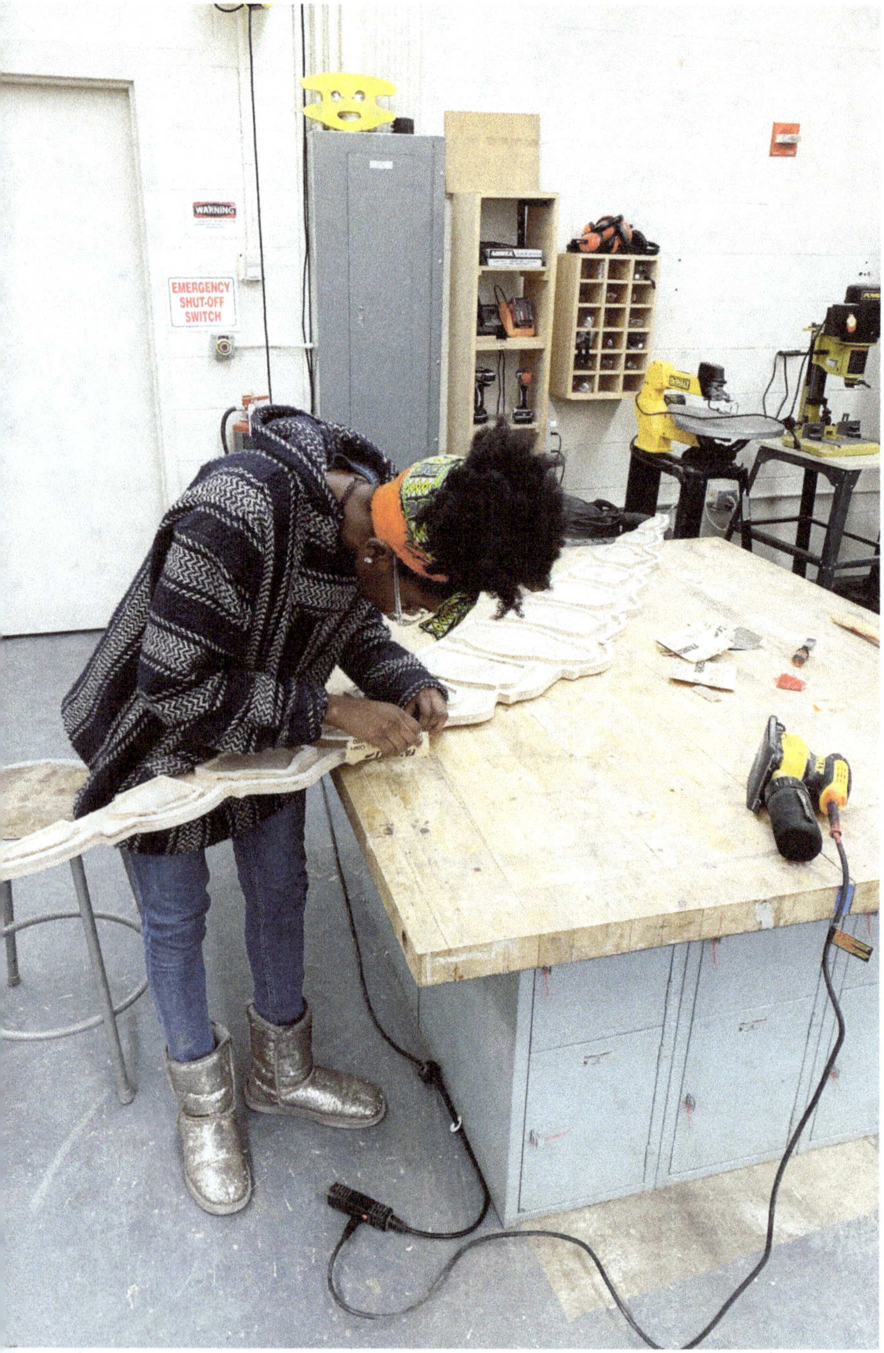
WARNING
EMERGENCY
SHUT-OFF
SWITCH

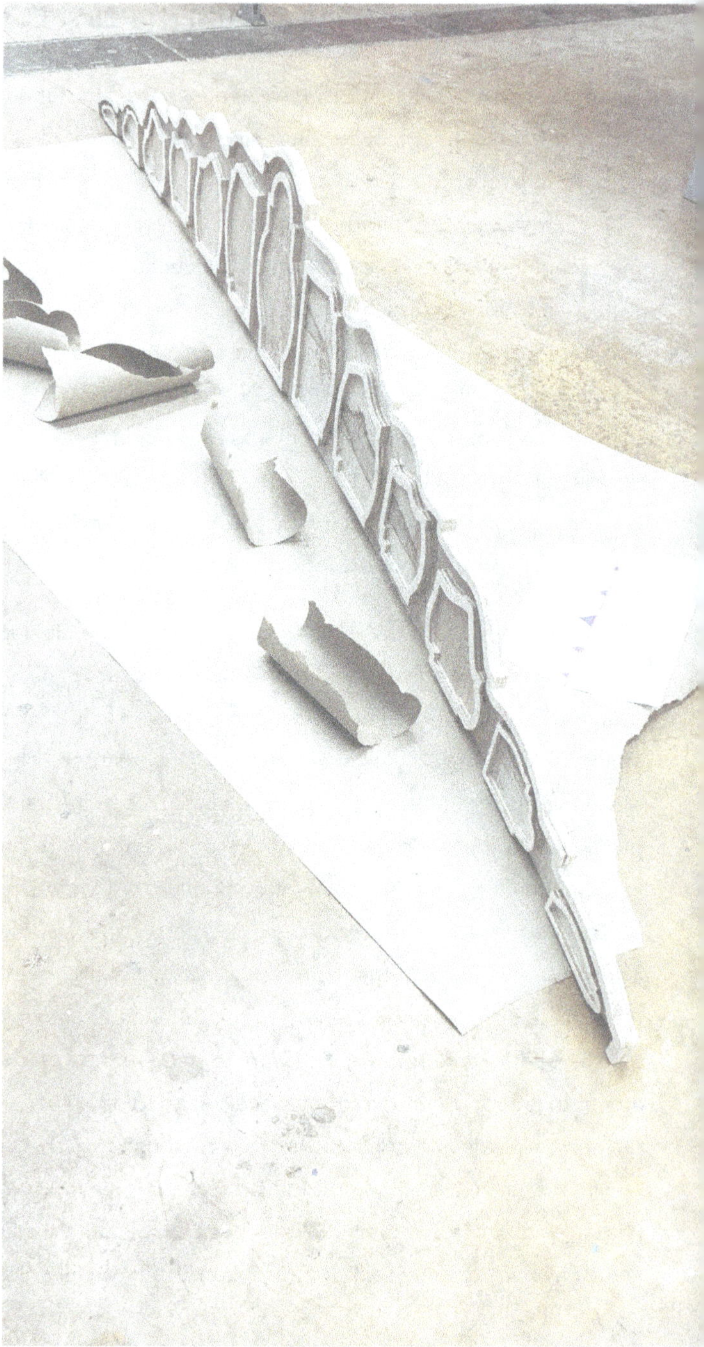

production

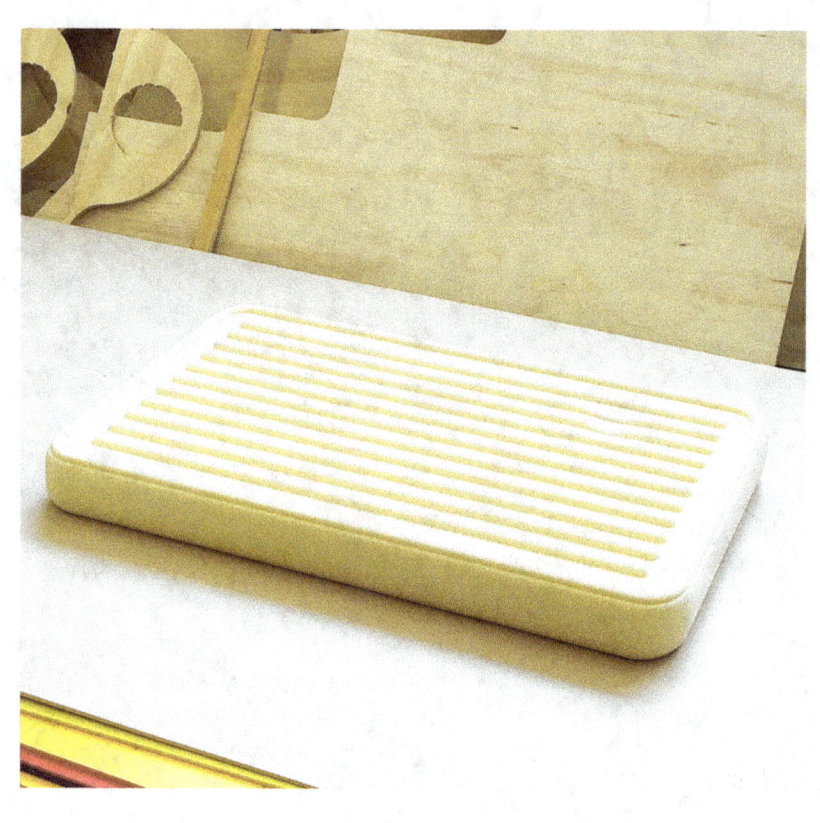

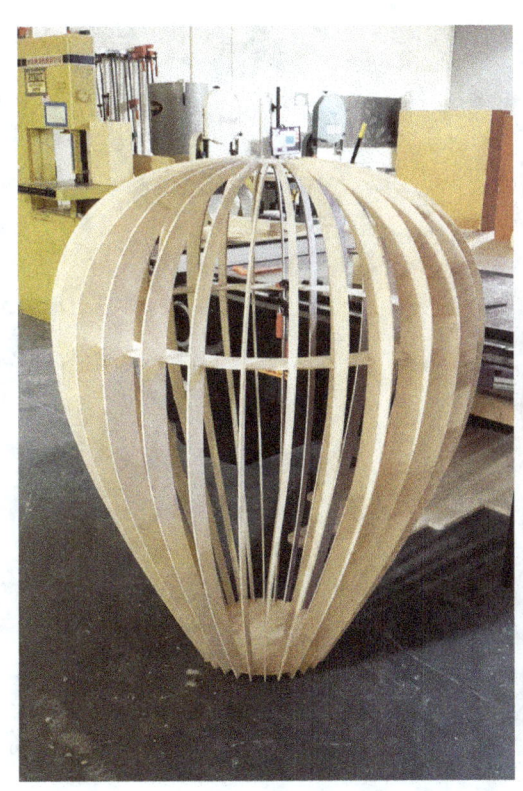
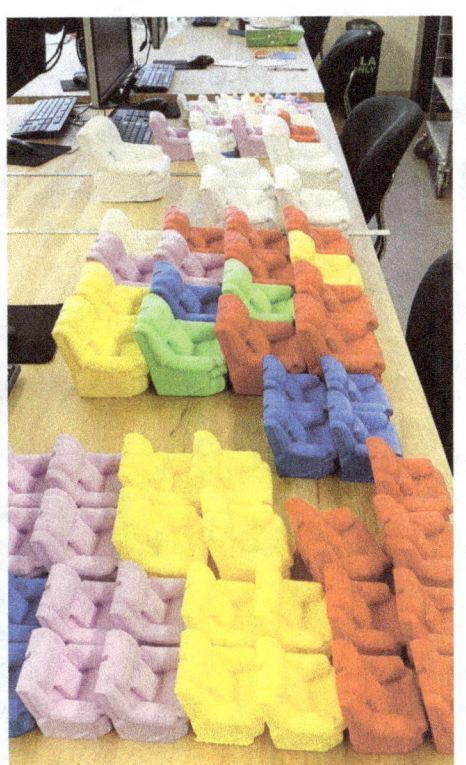
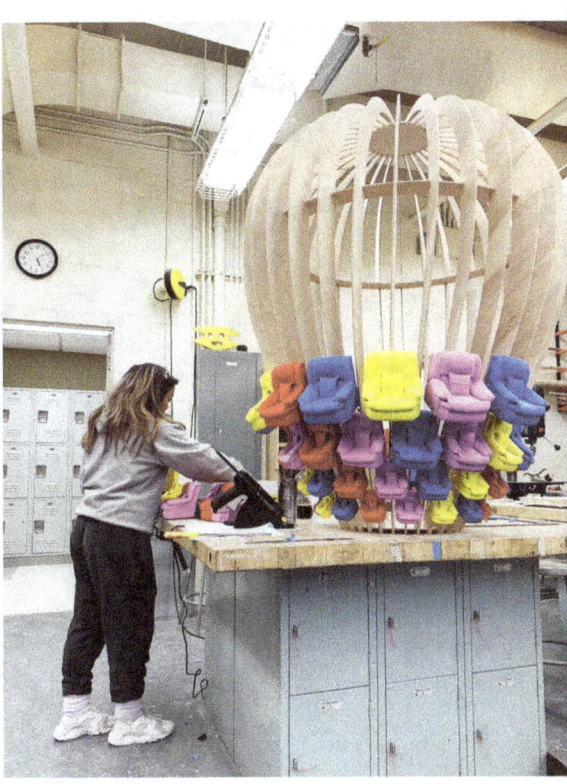

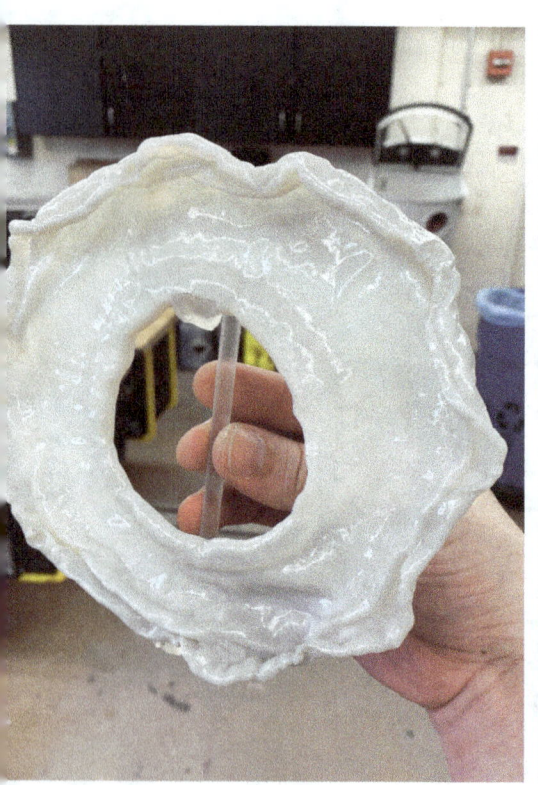
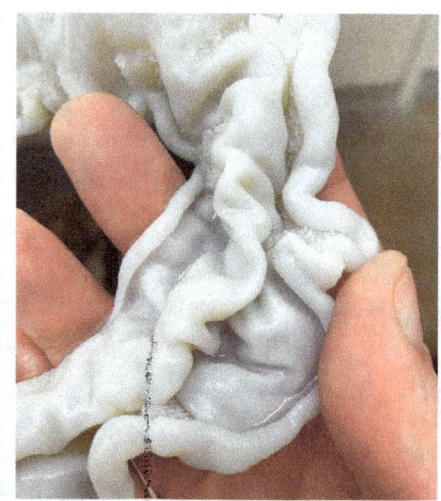
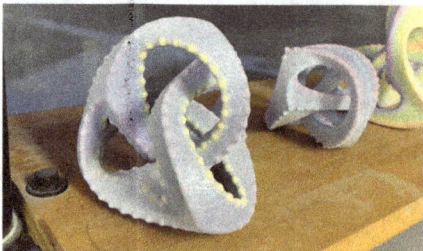
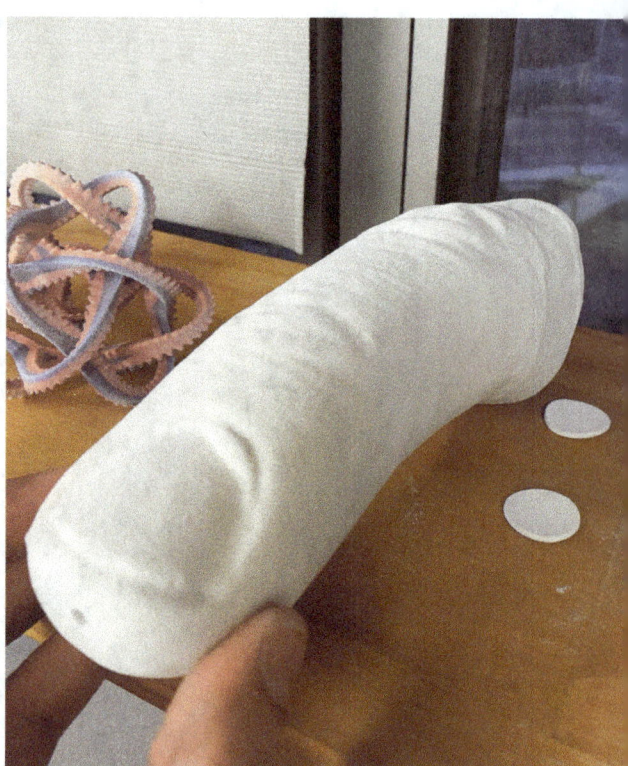

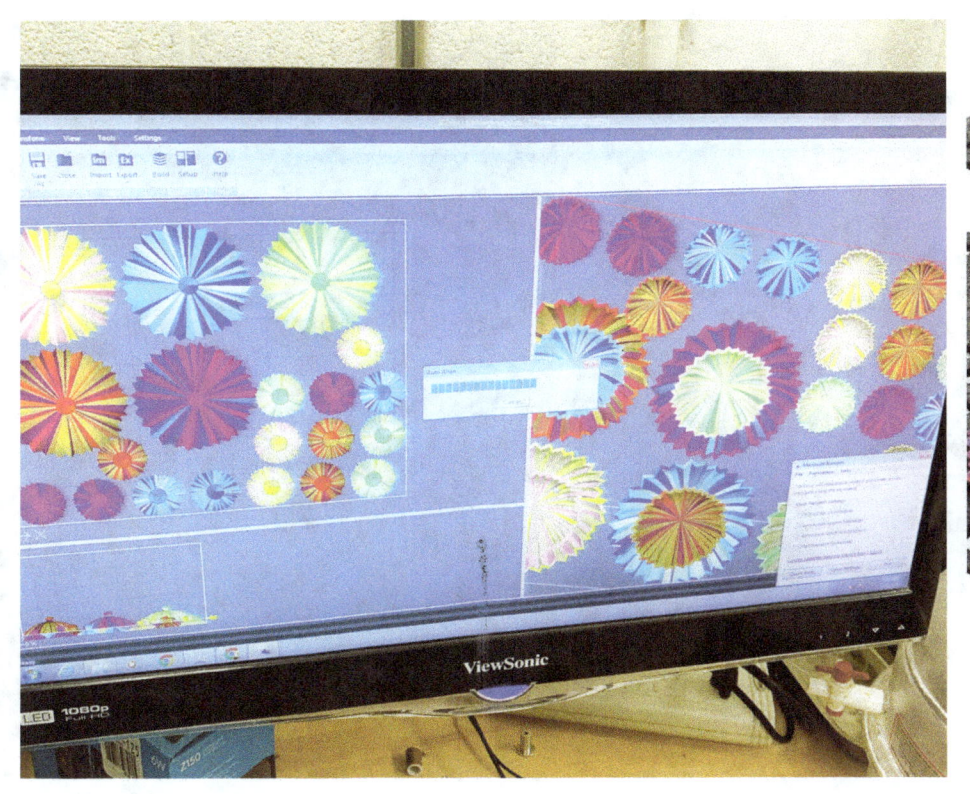

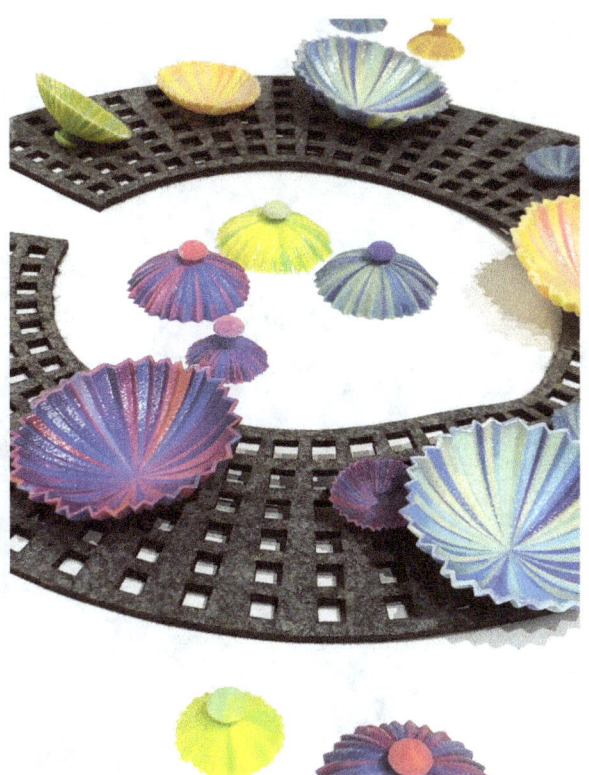

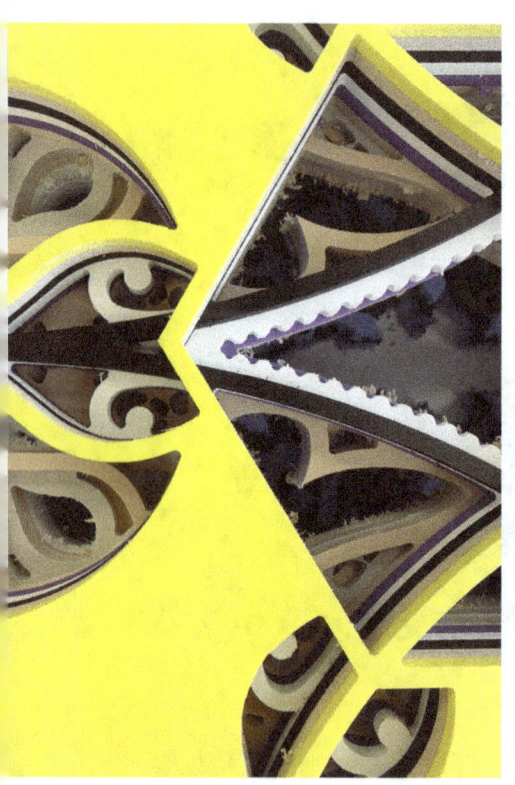
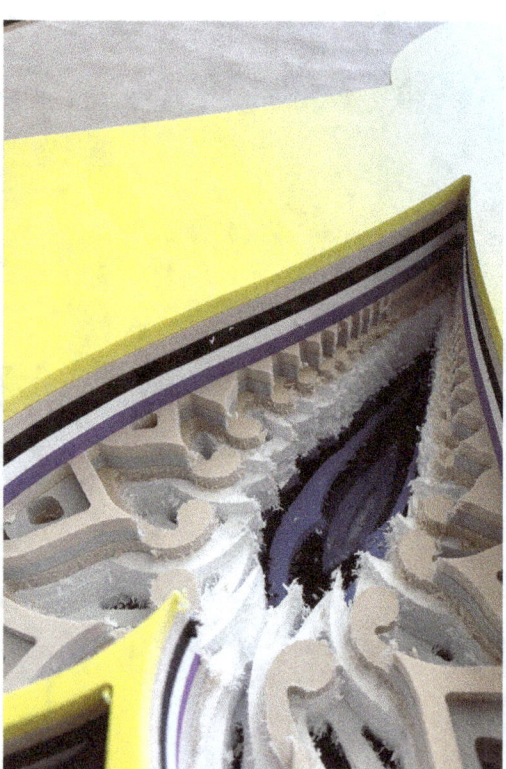
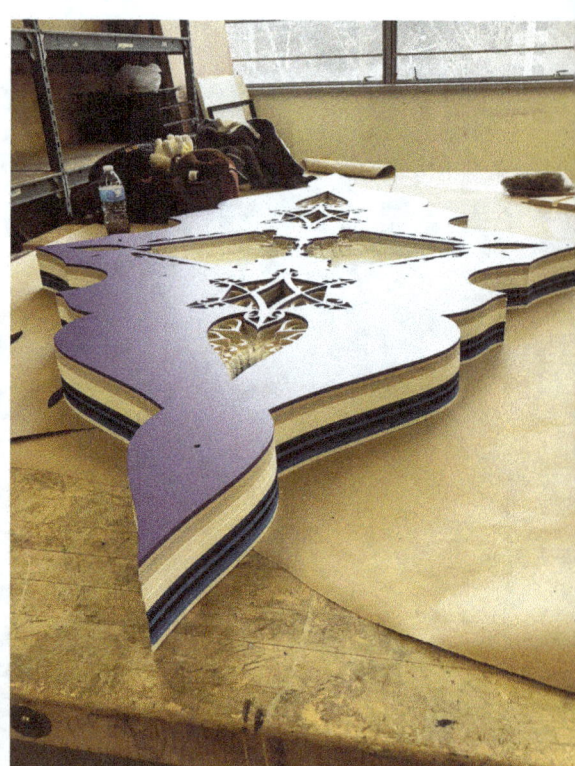

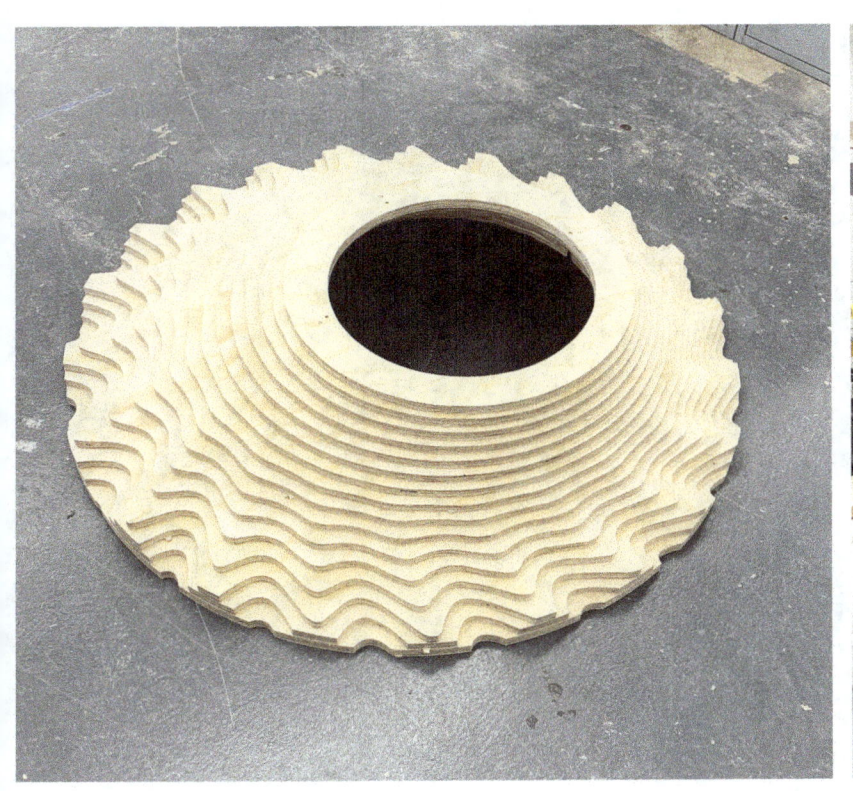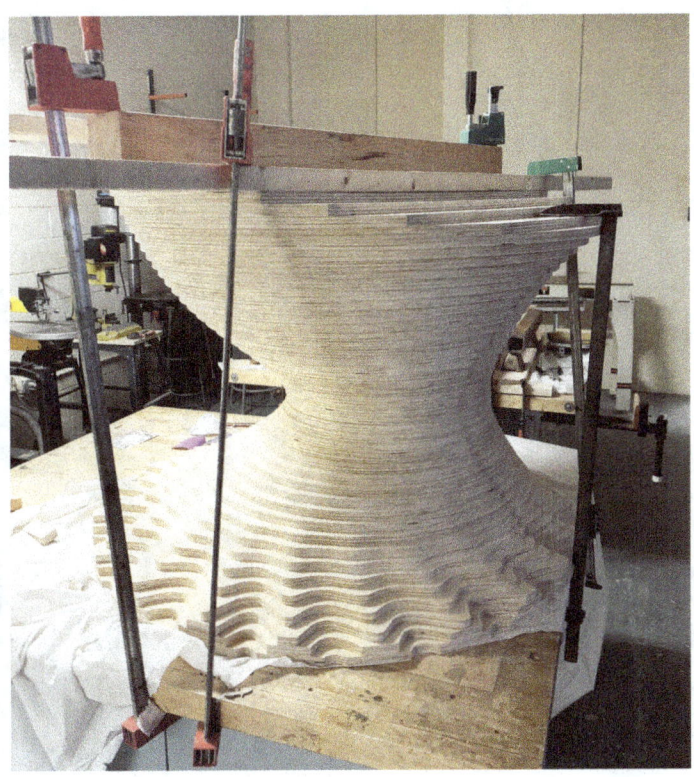

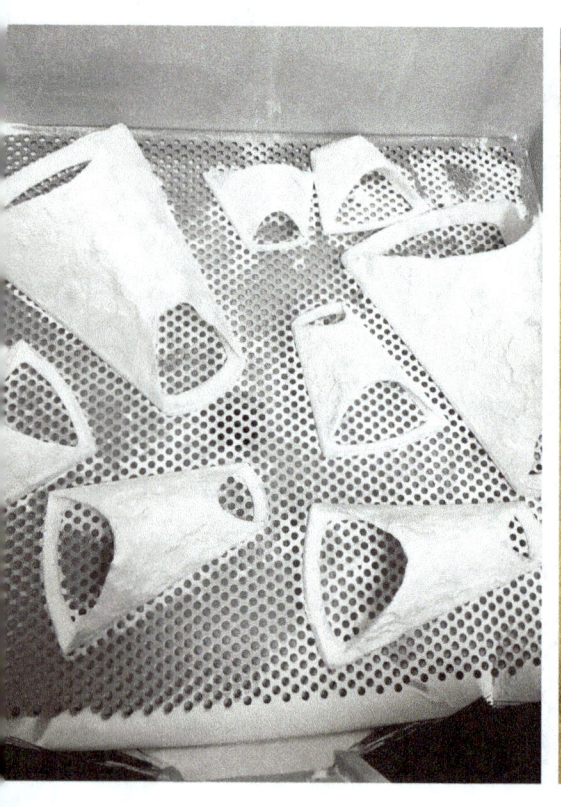
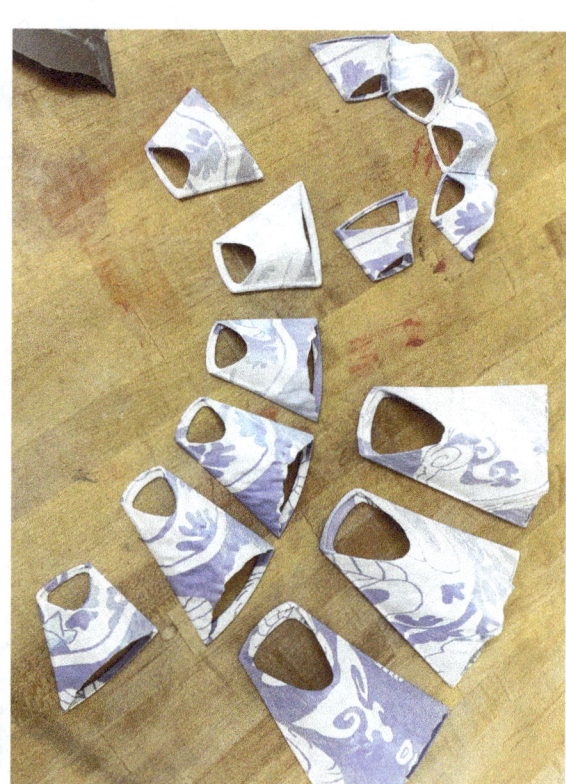
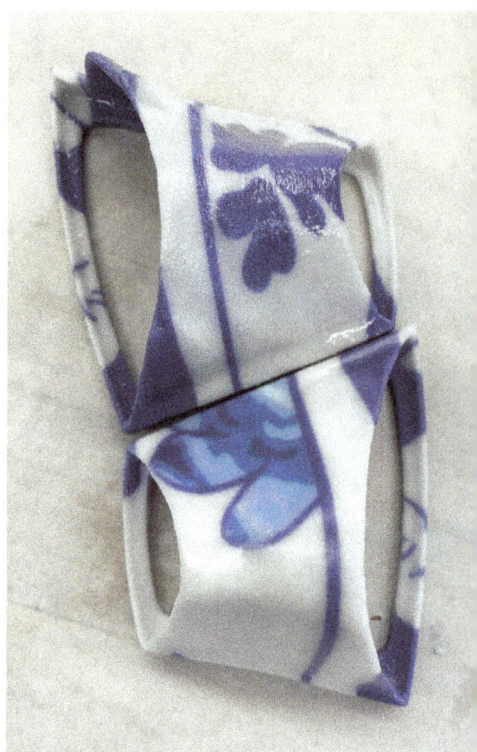

the production team

STUDENTS

Jacqueline Andrews

Marifel Bermudez

Kayla Boyer

Karima Hillard

Amy Ingram

Sterling Jennings

Amanda Kila

Richard Pence

Ellen Sisti

FACULTY & STAFF

Joshua DeMonte .... Curator

Elizabeth Donadio

Jon Lundak

Rachel Lundak

Michael Nashef

Mathew Sherwood

GALLERY STAFF

Erin Lehman, PhD .... Director of the Department of Art + Design, Art History - Art Education Galleries

J. Susan Isaacs, PhD .... Curator of the Department of Art + Design, Art History - Art Education Galleries

Venetia Zachary .... Director of the Visual Resource Center, Department of the Department of Art + Design, Art History, Art Education Galleries

Michael Bouyoucas .... Gallery Technician

You Wu .... Gallery Graduate Assistant

Briana Doyle .... Gallery Graduate Assistant